HOW TO WOW

With Illustrator

Ron Chan & Barbara Obermeier

Series Editor Jack Davis

Peachpit Press

How to Wow with Illustrator
Ron Chan and Barbara Obermeier

Peachpit Press
1249 Eighth Street
Berkeley, CA 94710
(510) 524-2178
(510) 524-2221 (fax)
Find us on the Web at www.peachpit.com.
To report errors, please send a note to errata@peachpit.com.

Peachpit Press is a division of Pearson Education.

Editor: Victor Gavenda
Development and Copy Editor: Anne Marie Walker
Production Editor: Hilal Sala
Technical Editor: Mordy Golding
Compositor: David Van Ness
Indexer: Patti Schiendelman
Proofreader: Dan J. Foster
Cover Design: Jack Davis
Interior Design: Jill Davis

ISBN 0-321-43454-4

9 8 7 6 5 4 3 2 1

Printed and bound in the United States of America

Acknowledgments

If not for Barbara Obermeier this book would not be in your hands, and I would be in a fetal position in the corner of my studio still contemplating the first chapter. Over the past few months as my friends and colleagues asked me how the book was going, the first words out of my mouth were always, "Thank God for Barb!" Her good humor, easy-going nature, experience, and knowledge were invaluable and much appreciated. My apologies for always asking you to write the tough stuff—but truthfully, I know when I'm out of my league.

I can't give enough thanks to my illustration colleagues and friends who so kindly provided the wonderful artwork you see in this book. Honestly, we didn't use all the artwork we were given because I just plain started to feel guilty. Many, many thanks to Steve Lyons, Isabelle Dervaux, David Flaherty, Joe Shoulak, Von Glitschka, Zach Trenholm, Steve Kearsley, and of course Craig Frazier, whose generosity never ceases to amaze me. My deep appreciation to my "Buzz" buddies: Jeffrey Pelo, man of too many talents; Gordon Studer, source of great envy and admiration; Timothy Cook, whose artwork makes me wonder why I even bother; Bryan Leister, a true Renaissance man; and last but not least, Bud Peen, friend, Giants buddy, source of many laughs, and a true artist. This book is dedicated to my Illustration family who are already so amazingly gifted that if each of them can pick up at least one tip from this book, I will be a happy man indeed.

Thanks to the gang at Peachpit who made this all possible: Nancy Ruenzel, for staying in touch after so many years; Rebecca Gulick, for giving birth to *two* babies and getting me together with Barb; Victor Gavenda, who kept the ball rolling when we were moving uphill; Hilal Sala and David Van Ness, whose hard work behind the scenes made the book look so good; and Anne Marie Walker, for the thankless nagging, cajoling, and skillful editing it took to get the book out the door. Thanks also to Jack and Jill Davis for trusting Barb and I to continue the wonderful *How-to-Wow* series you started: I hope we were able to keep up to the high standards you set.

My gratitude to Noreen Fukumori, Nana Mae's Organics, Metrovation, Hotel Healdsburg, the *San Francisco Chronicle*, Ken Linsteadt Architects, and the Marin Theatre Company for allowing me to use some of their work in this book.

Special thanks to Russell Brown who in the mid-80s let me play with a funny little program called Picasso inside a small room located in a nondescript office park of an unknown company called Adobe. My thanks also to Steve Broback and the denizens at the old Thunderlizard who started me on this road many years ago and introduced me to Sandee Cohen, who encouraged me to say yes to this book, and Mordy Golding, die-hard Mets fan, fountain of all Illustrator knowledge, tech editor extraordinaire, and good guy.

Finally, my never-ending appreciation and thanks to Nancy, Sami, and Nicky for putting up with the back of my head all this time while I wrote this book. After months and months of asking, "Isn't your book done yet?" I can finally say with great satisfaction and relief, "Yes."

—*Ron*

First and foremost, I would thank my coauthor Ron Chan. Besides his extensive knowledge of the inner workings of Illustrator, his great writing, and his fabulous illustrations, his sharp sense of humor and relaxed personality helped make this project a fun experience.

I would also like to thank all of the artists who so graciously allowed us to use their beautiful illustrations. Your work is inspiring and your immense talent enviable.

Thanks also go to Jack and Jill Davis, the proud parents of the *How-to-Wow* series. This series is like a breath of fresh air, and I feel fortunate to have made a small contribution to one of the books.

A heap load of gratitude is owed to the awesome editorial and production team at Peachpit. Thank you Rebecca and Victor for managing this book with endless patience. Kudos to Mordy Golding for your meticulous tech edit and Anne Marie Walker for your fantastic development and copy editing. Congratulations to Hilal Sala and David Van Ness for another beautifully laid out book. And thanks to Dan J. Foster for proofreading and Patti Schiendelman for indexing.

—*Barb*

Contents

6 ILLUSTRATOR AND THE WEB 162

7 INTEGRATING ILLUSTRATOR AND PHOTOSHOP 200

S SUPPLEMENT
S-1

Register this Book!

Stop! Don't turn this page until you've registered this book at the Peachpit Press Web site!

Benefits of registration include access to the actual Illustrator files for some of the projects described in the book. Feel free to open them up in Illustrator and compare them to the steps in the book. In many cases, however, you'll be able to follow along by using your existing artwork or even simple shapes. You'll also find 18 pages of supplemental projects in PDF form, whose contents are listed on the left side of this page. Remember that these materials are provided for your own personal use only. Please do not redistribute them.

To register, go to *www.peachpit.com/ bookstore/register.asp*. Enter the book's ISBN: 0321434544. You'll then be prompted to log in to peachpit.com or create an account if this is your first visit. After you register the book, a link to the supplemental content will be listed on your My Registered Books page. Come back to this page often for updated content, information about video tutorials, and more!

ILLUSTRATION BY RON CHAN

BEFORE FLASH, PHOTOSHOP, and even the World Wide Web, there was Adobe Illustrator. The most widely used vector drawing program available today, Illustrator is a powerful program both in depth and breadth. For some it can be slightly intimidating to start working with. Unlike Photoshop where you start with some content, usually a photograph, Illustrator starts with a blank, white artboard and requires that you create your own content from scratch.

Although this is not a reference book (many fine books are on the market—including Mordy Golding's *Real World Illustrator CS2* [Peachpit Press, 2006]—that go over the basics and give you a

detailed description of each and every feature), we quickly go over the fundamentals of Illustrator. For example, we discuss tasks like setting up a new document the right way and establishing your color management. From there, we take it up a notch and show you how to become a wiz with the Pen tool and gain an understanding of the intricacies of paths of all sorts. Once you get comfortable with the fundamentals, we move to the meat of the book and the main objective—productivity.

Our How to Wow Goal

In researching this book, we talked to many, many Illustrator users and asked them what they would want to learn; we were struck by a common response. No matter how experienced, famous, or successful the person, none thought they were "experts" at using the application with which they lived and breathed almost every day of their working lives. Everyone knew what they needed to know to produce beautiful and creative pieces of artwork in Illustrator, but nothing more. It made perfect sense to us though; Illustrator has become such a complex application, how could anyone know it all? Our goal for this book became not to show you how to do a neon glow around text or use a filter that you might use once in your lifetime, but instead to make you more productive. So we focused on introducing shortcuts, workarounds, and methods that mesh with your existing workflow but don't alter it. And we concentrated our effort on making your illustration tasks easier and more fun in less time.

"Frustration" is not in our vocabulary. We're here to guide you through bumps in the road of becoming a more knowledgeable Illustrator user. We'll show you some tips and techniques that we've learned by using Illustrator for our own illustration and design projects.

What's in It for You?

As with most activities in life, once you're comfortable with the fundamentals, you usually get hungry for refinement and productivity. Take baseball for example. Once you learn the rules of the game, become familiar with the equipment, and play a few games, you're ready to improve your swing and turn that double play. Using Illustrator is no different. We don't want to teach you how to play baseball. You already know

ILLUSTRATION BY DAVID FLAHERTY

how to do that. We want to help you get to first base faster and look better while you're doing it. If you're anything like us, learning a few tips to make your digital illustrating smoother and quicker is well worth a small investment.

How to Use This Book and the Downloadable Supplements

We know we're not the boss of you, but please start this book by registering your purchase at Peachpit's Web site. Benefits of registration include access to the actual Illustrator files for some of the projects described in the book, as well as 18 pages of supplemental projects in PDF form. Remember that these materials are provided for your own personal use only. Please do not redistribute them. For more information about registering your book, see the last page of the Table of Contents (just flip back two pages).

Next, dive in to the book itself and start by reading the first chapter. Chapter 1 gives you some fundamentals that make your illustrating life a little easier. After you've perused that chapter, feel free to jump to any other chapter that suits your fancy. 🕮

ILLUSTRATION BY ZACH TRENHOLM

1

PROGRAM FOUNDATIONS

*Getting Started,
Saving Time, and
Being More Productive*

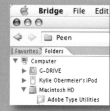

A S ENTICING AS IT IS to buy a book, flip through its crisp, new pages and pounce on a page that has seduced you with its gorgeous illustrations, we beg you to show a little restraint. It's not that we're rigid linear disciplinarians who demand that you start on the first page and end on the last page or risk having your file blow up into some digital wasteland. It's just that Chapter 1 contains information we feel will help you get started in the most efficient way. Once you've gotten off to this great start, we'll give you some shortcuts and time-saving techniques. And if you're like us, with regard to computers, anytime you find the words "time" and "saving" together rather than "time" and "consuming," it warrants your attention. Have you ever said, "This should only take a couple minutes," only to find yourself an hour later still tackling that cantankerous compound path or trying to get your color print to look acceptable? This chapter will enable you to save enough time to go out and smell the roses—the actual flowers, not the ones on your screen.

Setting Up with Purpose

Thomas Edison once said, "Results! Why, man I have gotten a lot of results. I know several thousand things that won't work." We can all relate to that. Often, getting what you want at the tail end is predicated by what you do at the very beginning. Setting up your file for your particular workflow or desired output is often half the battle when trying to complete a problem-free project. We'll also give you information on creating custom workspaces and startup files so you'll have the optimum interface for your chosen workflow.

Getting a Handle on Color

Not getting consistent color is the proverbial thorn in the side of many artists and designers. Managing color starts with setting up an optimum working environment, correctly specifying your software settings and then your file, and getting good final output, whether onscreen or on paper. This section gives you an abridged explanation of the color management process, including understanding profiles and workspaces, and what to do when Illustrator alerts you that your file has a mismatched or missing color profile.

Navigating and Saving Time

Once you've set up your file and workspace, we'll give you information on how to use Adobe Bridge to navigate and manage your digital assets. Yes, there are issues with Bridge. There's no denying that it can be slow. But if you give it a chance, you may find that Bridge can also be a powerful partner in keeping you organized. We'll also give you an array of tips that we've found handy when creating an illustration or design, such as making calculations within palettes and using a blend to create a color palette.

Set Up Your File

You can set up a file in many ways in Illustrator. Some people keep everything on a single layer, whereas others feel the need to separate every piece of art into individual layers, layer groupings, and sublayers. The setup that follows is a way to set up your file easily and logically but with a great degree of flexibility.

1. Create a New Document

The first and most important step when creating a new document is to define a document color mode. Choosing a Color Mode in the New Document dialog automatically loads default color swatches relevant to either CMYK or RGB, depending on the color mode you choose. If you decide to change the color mode after you start working on the file, the default color swatches won't change. You can of course load the default color swatches manually, but you will have to do that every time you open the document.

2. Define Your Artboard

Select an artboard size that provides you with a lot of extra space. Tabloid size is usually sufficient for most projects unless of course your final size is 11 x 17. Don't be too concerned about setting the artboard to the final size of the output; we will set the crop area to take care of that later. However, there are some instances when you'll want to set the artboard to the exact size of your finished piece—artwork or page designs with no bleed for instance. For more on the artboard, see "Artboard vs. Bounding Boxes vs. Crop Marks vs. Crop Area" later in this chapter.

T I P

Color Settings and Profile. An important but often overlooked part of setting up your file is choosing the correct color setting and profile. Many times whole files are built, colored, and rendered, only for users to find out that the final color output is totally different than intended because they forgot to choose a color setting and profile. This is true for both print and Web output. Don't let it happen to you! Read "Color Management" later in this chapter for a clear (meaning not from an engineer's point of view) explanation of this topic.

C A U T I O N

Changing Color Modes. If you change color modes in the middle of your project, the color values in your file will also change. For instance, if you start in CMYK color mode with a fill color of 40%C, 0%M, 100%Y, and 0%K, and then change to RGB color mode, your fill color will be converted to 38.82%C, 0%M, 98.82%Y, and .78%K. Changing your color mode back to CMYK will not convert the color values back to their original state.

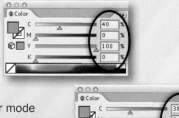

3. Place a Scanned Image

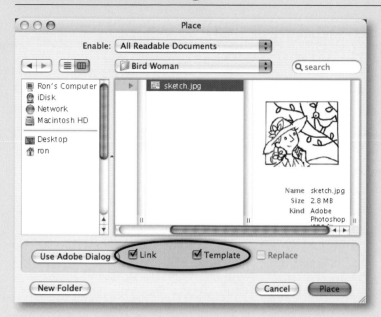

If you are using a scanned image as the basis for your illustration, import it into your document by choosing File > Place and navigating to the location where the file is stored on your hard drive. In the Place dialog box, select the Link check box, which will create a reference to the location of the scanned image on your hard drive. If you move the location of the scanned file at a later time, the link will be broken and the image will not appear in your Illustrator file. You can also choose to deselect the Link check box, which will

embed the image file into your Illustrator file. However, depending on the image file size, this could increase your Illustrator file size considerably and hinder the application's performance. In addition, select the Template check box to place the scanned image into a template layer. A template layer is very useful as a tracing guide when building your objects on top of it, and it is nonprinting. Template layers can be toggled on or off for viewing by using Cmd (Ctrl)-Shift-W.

4. Create a Matte Layer

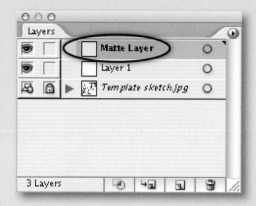

As you work on your illustration or design, it's helpful to be able to see how the artwork will appear in its final trimmed size without the distraction of extraneous paths and objects. In the Layers palette, create a new layer on top of all your other layers. On this new layer, create a "matte" as shown in the "Create a Matte Layer" project later in this chapter.

T I P

Turn Up the Template Layer Contrast.
In the Layer Options dialog box, double-click the actual layer in the Layers palette and change the template layer opacity to 20–30% instead of the default 50%. Reducing the opacity of the template layer makes the scanned image appear fainter, so the paths that you draw on top of it stand out more clearly.

5. Make a Crop Area

The last step before you start your illustration or design is to create a crop area. Not to be confused with crop marks (Filter > Create > Crop Marks), which are used to draw "tick" marks on the page, a crop area actually defines the physical area that can be exported or saved to Photoshop, PDF, JPEG, or any number of file formats.

The biggest advantage to using a crop area instead of confining your artwork to the artboard size is the flexibility a crop area provides (see "Artboard vs. Bounding Boxes vs. Crop Marks vs. Crop Area" later in this chapter). For instance, if you decide to move the crop area or make the area larger or smaller, just release the crop area and move the area instead of changing the artboard size and then

moving the entire artwork (in which case you'll inevitably forget to select or unlock an object and then have to undo and start all over again).

Unlock the Matte layer and select the path that defines the "crop." Be sure to click on the actual path, not the center of the "doughnut hole." Use Cmd (Ctrl)-C to copy the path to the clipboard. Deselect the path and then choose Edit > Paste in Front (Cmd [Ctrl]-F) to place a copy of the path in the exact position of the original "crop" rectangle. Next, choose Object > Crop Area > Make. Now when you export your file, the artwork outside of your crop area will not show up, and you'll have an exact image size ready for placement in InDesign, Photoshop, Dreamweaver, and so on.

6. Create a Bleed

Creating a bleed area (extra artwork outside of the matte area) after the illustration or design is finished is also very easily done using this workflow method. You'll first need to release the crop area you just made (Object > Crop Area > Release) to create a new crop area that incorporates the bleed.

Working with the same path you created to use for your Matte layer, choose File > Copy and then Edit > Paste in Front. With the path still selected, choose Object > Path > Offset Path. Enter the desired amount of bleed into the Offset field and click OK **A**. Instead of using Offset Path you can also specify the bleed area using the Transform palette **B** (see "Calculation Inside Dialog Boxes and Palettes" later in this chapter) to resize the path. With the path still selected, choose Object > Crop Area > Make to create the new crop area incorporating the bleed.

Athough your bleed and final output size is set with the crop area, visually you are still only seeing your trim area because of the Matte layer. ▥

CAUTION

Only One Crop Area Allowed.
Remember, you can only have one crop area per file! Making a crop area is not like making crop marks (Filter > Create > Crop Marks), which are strokes and do not define a physical area.

Create a Matte Layer

A Matte layer—a more versatile layer clipping mask—makes it easy to view your artwork the way it will appear in its final state.

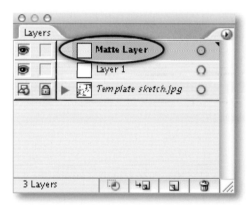

TIP

Multiple Mattes. Matte layers are also handy if you have more than one piece of artwork on the artboard that needs to be masked out, such as multiple business cards or spot illustrations. For more about how to add to a compound path, see "Tip: Adding to a Compound Path" in "Compound Paths within Compound Paths" later in this chapter.

1. Create a New Layer

As mentioned earlier, creating a Matte layer helps you view your artwork the way it will be seen in its final form by hiding any extraneous elements that fall outside the matte area. Although layer clipping masks (see Chapter 3, "Masks and Blend Effects") can serve a similar purpose, the downside of layer clipping masks is that they only apply to one layer, so if you want to set up your file with multiple layers, you'll instead need to work with sublayers, which are not as fast or intuitive. Setting up a Matte layer lets you work on the top level of the Layers palette and create layers and objects that will be visually cropped out as you make them. Most important, the Matte layer can be viewed or hidden with a click of the Show/Hide button in the Layers palette.

In the Layers palette, create a new layer and name it "Matte Layer." Make sure this layer is on top of all your other layers in the stacking order.

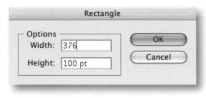

2. Draw a Rectangle

Using the Rectangle tool, click the artboard to open the Rectangle dialog box and manually enter the final size of your project. You can also click and drag to create a rectangle of the final project size. Fill the rectangle that you just created with any color. If you're using a scan, position your matte rectangle to align with the scan.

3. Draw Another Rectangle

Using the Rectangle tool, create a second rectangle 2 to 3 inches larger than the rectangle you just created. Cut this larger rectangle to the clipboard (File > Cut or Cmd [Ctrl]-X), select the first rectangle, and choose Edit > Paste in Back (or press Cmd [Ctrl]-B) to place the larger shape behind the "crop" rectangle.

4. Make a Compound Path

Select both shapes and choose Object > Compound Path > Make (Cmd [Ctrl]-8) or use the Exclude shape mode in the Pathfinder palette to create a "doughnut," which will serve as a mask or matte for the artwork underneath. Change the resulting compound path or compound shape's color to white, black, or gray if you prefer, and then lock your new Matte layer.

5. View Your New Matte Layer

The result is a Matte layer that hides any extraneous artwork on the layers below it without modifying the objects or paths on those layers. Keep the Matte layer on top of the layer stacking order. Locking the layer prevents you from inadvertently selecting the artwork on that layer when working. Unlike clipping layer masks, which can't be hidden, you can just click the Show/Hide button of the Matte layer in the Layers palette to view your artwork with or without the matte. ▥

T I P

Layer Text Intelligently. Place text on its own layer to prevent problems with screen redraw and object selection. If your illustration has a lot of text, scrolling in your document will be sluggish. It is also difficult to select items behind a text block. More important, placing text on its own top-level layer can help prevent text becoming rasterized due to transparency flattening. If text is on a separate layer, you can avoid these issues by hiding the layer until needed or locking it so the text block can't be selected by mistake.

Layers

		Matte Layer	○
		Text	○
		Details	○
		Artwork	○
		Background	○
		Template sketch.jpg	○

6 Layers

Creating Custom Workspaces

In Illustrator a workspace includes your illustration window (where you draw), your toolbox, palette, and menus. But you don't have to settle for Illustrator's default workspace. You can customize your workspace to fit your personal workflow. In fact, you can create multiple custom workspaces tailored to different types of work, such as Web or print, or to individual projects or clients. Display only what you need and cut the clutter from your workspace.

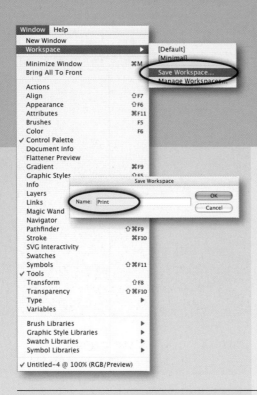

Set Up a Custom Workspace

Open, combine, and arrange the palettes you want to use for a particular project, client, or type of work. Once you have your desired configuration, choose Window > Workspace > Save Workspace. Name your workspace and click OK. Your workspace is now ready to load at any time.

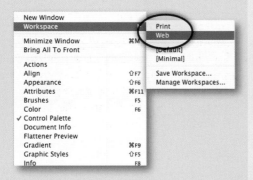

Switch Workspaces

To switch to a different workspace, simply choose Window > Workspace and choose your desired workspace from the submenu. The [Minimal] workspace will display only the Tools palette and the menu bar. The [Default] workspace will display the Tools palette, menu bar, Control palette, and the Appearance, Color, Layers, Stroke, and Swatches palettes. Note that any bracketed setting cannot be deleted from Illustrator.

Manage Workspaces

If you need to rename, delete, or duplicate a workspace, choose Window > Workspace > Manage Workspaces. In the dialog box, select the workspace you want to rename, type in the new name in the field, and then click OK. To delete the workspace, click the Delete button. To duplicate the workspace, select it and click New. ▥

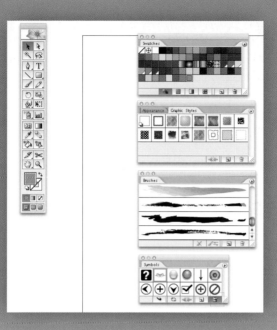

Set Up a Custom Startup File

Want to take it a step further? Create your own custom startup file.

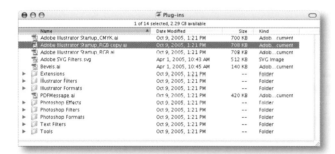

1. Make a Copy of the Original

Before you create a custom startup file, you may want to make a copy of the original startup file since you will be overwriting the original. If you inadvertently delete a startup file, don't worry. Illustrator will automatically create a new default the next time the application is launched. For both Macintosh and Windows, you'll find the startup files in the Plug-ins folder in the Adobe Illustrator Applications folder.

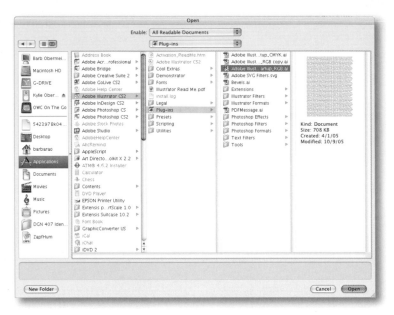

2. Open the Startup File

Double-click to open either the
Adobe Illustrator Startup_CMYK.ai
or Adobe Illustrator Startup_RGB.ai file.

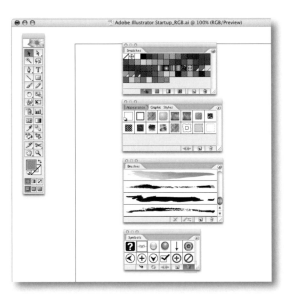

3. Customize Your Palettes

Customize your palettes by deleting
any color swatches, gradients, patterns, graphic and text styles, brushes,
and symbols you don't want. Create or
import any new desired color swatches,
gradients, patterns, styles, brushes, or
symbols. Note that you can also change
the default font by editing the Normal
Paragraph Style in the Paragraph Styles
palette.

4. Specify Your Viewing Preference

In the View menu, define your default
viewing preferences. Also, establish
your desired ruler origin—where your
zeros appear on your rulers for height
and width.

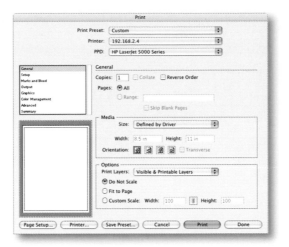

5. Specify Your Print Options

Choose File > Print to specify your default print settings in the Print dialog box.

6. Delete Unwanted Actions

Choose Window > Actions to delete any unwanted actions and add any new actions.

7. Save the Custom Startup File

Once you've completed your configuration, choose File > Save As and be sure to save the file in the Plug-ins folder in the Illustrator Applications folder. Also, be sure not to change the name of the file.

8. Restart Illustrator

Choose Illustrator > Quit Illustrator, or File > Exit in Windows. Restart Illustrator to load the new startup file. ▥

Shortcuts to Save You Time

As much as you love sitting in front of your computer working in Illustrator, there must be times when you wish you had an extra 15 minutes to enjoy the sunset or share some quality time with your kids. While the following tips might not give you those 15 minutes right away, they will at least get you started in the right direction.

Calculation Inside Dialog Boxes and Palettes

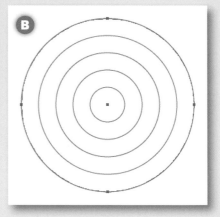

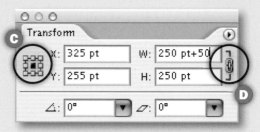

You can use mathematical operations in most palettes (for example, Control, Transform, Text) that accept numbers to change the value of an object's size, position, rotation, and so on. Just place your cursor into an entry field, enter a math operation (+, −, /, *) into the dialog box with a number, and then press Enter. The object will change based on the result of the calculation. This technique comes in very handy for exacting work such as setting up slices for the Web (see Chapter 6, "Illustrator and the Web").

It's also important to note that you can mix and match different measurement settings as well. For example, you can input **4in + 3p5** and Illustrator will do the conversion *and* the math.

Remember, when changing an object from within the Transform and Control palettes, the origin point is specified by the reference point **A**.

In the Transform palette, using a math operation or a calculation and pressing the Option (Alt) key while pressing Enter will make a duplicate of the object.

In this example **B**, we selected a circle and entered +50 into the Width field in the Transform palette. We clicked the center reference point **C** and the Constrain Width and Height Proportions button **D**, and then pressed Option (Alt) while pressing Enter. This produced a second, concentric circle spaced 25 pt from the original circle.

Change Units Shortcut

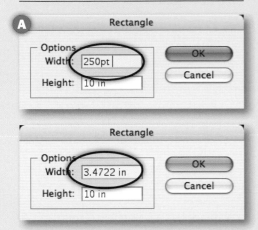

Change Arrow Key Distance

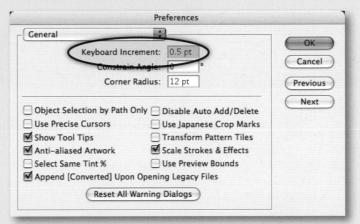

Inches, points, picas, pixels—it seems that you never have the right unit of measurement when you need it. Here are a couple of tips that will help you change your unit of measurement without going through the Preferences dialog box.

Press Cmd-Option (Ctrl-Alt)-Shift-U ("U" for units) and the unit measurement preference will cycle through inches, millimeters, centimeters, pixels, points, and picas.

In any dialog box **A** that requires a unit of measure, you can "force" it to accept any unit if you type it in. For instance, you can type *in* or *"* for inches, *p* for picas, *pt* for points, *px* for pixels, *mm* for millimeters, or *cm* for centimeters.

Using the arrow key(s) is an easy way to move an object around the page. For example, you might want to nudge an object in very small increments (for example, .05 pt) to align it exactly to another object. Or you might want to match the leading of a text paragraph so that you can move objects up and down in a design while keeping it aligned to the baseline of the text.

An easy habit to learn is to just press Cmd (Ctrl)-K (which opens your Preferences dialog box), type in an arrow key distance, and then press Enter or Return. Since the Keyboard Increment is the first highlighted entry when you open the window, with a little practice you can change the arrow key increment and press Enter almost as fast as the time it takes for the dialog box to open.

Additional options for using the arrow keys:

- Holding down the Shift key while using the arrow keys will move an object ten times the value of the keyboard increment.

- Holding down the Option (Alt) key while using the arrow keys will create a copy of the selected object(s) and then move the copied object(s) at the same time.

Paste in Front/Back

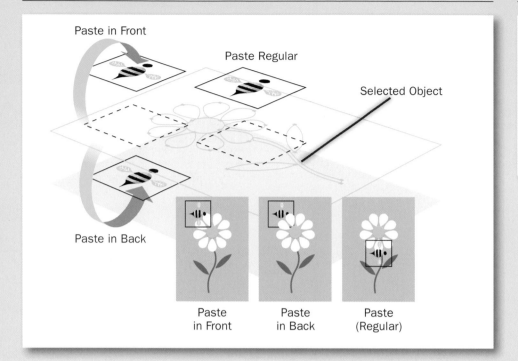

Paste in Front

Paste Regular

Selected Object

Paste in Back

Paste
in Front

Paste
in Back

Paste
(Regular)

Quick Join

The Edit > Paste in Front/Paste in Back (Cmd [Ctrl]-F and Cmd [Ctrl]-B) commands are the most useful stacking tools in Illustrator. Unlike the normal Paste command (Cmd [Ctrl]-V), which places an object from the clipboard to the center of the viewing area, Paste in Front/Back will place the object at the same *x, y* coordinates from which it was cut or copied. If an object is selected before pasting, Paste in Front/Back will place the object in the clipboard in the correct stacking relationship to the selected object. This method is a very intuitive way to work, since arranging objects is merely a question of deciding if the "nose" should go in front or back of the "face" (for the record, it's in front...)

Not only do the Paste in Front/Back commands make the Bring to Front command in the Arrange menu (Object > Arrange) obsolete, but they also do away with ever having to deal with the seeming hundreds of sublayers in the Layers palette.

> **T I P**
>
> **Paste Into Groups.** The Paste in Front/Back commands are also powerful tools for pasting into grouped objects, compound paths, and especially masks. For a more detailed explanation of masks, see Chapter 3.

When closing the paths of an object, instead of selecting or highlighting the two open points with the Direct Selection tool, use the Selection tool (solid arrow). Or use the Direct Selection tool and Option (Alt)-click to highlight all the points of the path/object. Then press Cmd (Ctrl)-J and the path/object will close by itself. Although this might only save you seconds, considering the number of paths in a typical Illustrator file, the time can add up quickly.

Smart Guides

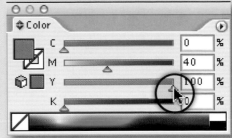

Stupid (But Useful!) Color Trick

You can easily align objects using View > Snap to Point (unless you are in Pixel Preview mode where the option is called Snap to Pixel). With this option enabled and an object selected, Snap to Point changes the cursor from black to hollow when it moves on top of another point where you want your object to align, "snapping" the points to each other. However, sometimes if you zoom in very closely you'll find that the objects/points are not exactly aligned as they should be. This is because Snap to Point actually uses the cursor's position to "snap" to the point, *not* the object or anchor point's position you are moving.

If you require accuracy for how your objects align to each other, using Smart Guides is a much better way to go. Not only will Smart Guides give you true

point-to-point alignment, but Smart Guides will also align segments and objects at 90- and 45-degree angles (or any angle specified in the Preferences dialog). This feature is especially useful in Web design when creating Illustrator slices (see Chapter 6), where you need to align objects to the exact pixel.

Unfortunately, Smart Guides can also become incredibly annoying during normal drawing workflow because words, lines, and angles appear and disappear as you work, making it look like they are constantly flashing at you. However, if you remember that Cmd (Ctrl)-U toggles Smart Guides mode on and off, you'll find yourself using this feature more and more.

If you need to make a proportional variation of the color in the Color palette, hold down the Cmd (Ctrl) *or* Shift key, and then click and drag the slider arrow. The overall increments of the color will change proportionally higher or lower depending on which direction you drag the slider arrow.

Too Many Objects

ILLUSTRATION BY JEFFREY PELO

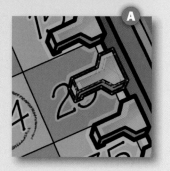

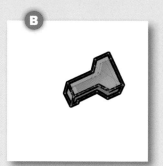

Number Value Shortcut with Arrows

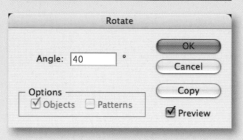

Working in Illustrator sometimes means creating hundreds of paths and objects. After a while, trying to work on a single object in this visual haystack becomes daunting and confusing. You can choose to bring the object you are working on to a new layer and then hide the other layers, but that usually means your object will move out of the stacking order, so this option may be impractical (especially for complex illustrations). Holding down the Shift key while selecting the surrounding objects and then hiding them is time-consuming and tedious.

An easier and much faster way to work is to hide all the unnecessary objects on the artboard. This is simply done by selecting the object **A** you would like to work on and pressing Cmd-Option (Ctrl-Alt)-Shift-3. This will hide *all* the objects *except* the one selected, enabling you to work on the object without the surrounding objects getting in your way **B**. To bring all the hidden objects back into view, just press Cmd-Option (Ctrl-Alt)-3.

T I P

Lock All. You can also lock all but selected objects by pressing Cmd-Option (Ctrl-Alt)-Shift-2. This will prevent you from selecting or editing all the other objects on your artboard and allow you to work with only the objects you chose.

A trick to quickly change the number value of any Transformation (Scale, Rotate, Shear, Move) dialog box and Color palette is to insert your cursor into a field and press the up arrow key to increase the value or the down arrow key to decrease the value. Holding down the Shift key while pressing the up/down arrow keys will change the value in increments of ten *except* in the Move dialog box, where the amount of change depends on the current unit of measurement.

For instance, if your unit of measurement is inches, holding down the Shift key while pressing the up/down arrow keys in the Move dialog box will move your object in increments of 1 inch. This also holds true for picas (1 pica) and centimeters (1 centimeter). Millimeters and pixels change by a factor of ten. Points, however, change by six.

Artboard vs. Bounding Boxes vs. Crop Marks vs. Crop Area

Before you get started with a new document, you need to learn about how the artboard, bounding boxes, crop marks, and the crop area work.

Artboard

ILLUSTRATION BY ZACH TRENHOLM

You create an artboard when you choose Letter, Tabloid, or Legal in the New Document dialog box. The main thing to remember about the artboard is that anything outside of it will not print. Even if you specify a crop area, if it falls outside the dimensions of the artboard, Illustrator will not recognize it. Basically, the artboard is your universe, and you can't go beyond it. Our recommendation for the artboard size is to make it about 2–3 inches larger than the final size of your artwork, which gives you plenty of room to work with. Choose Letter or Tabloid size if the final size of your artwork fits comfortably within those dimensions. Specifying the artboard to the exact size of your finished piece works when you are creating a document with no bleed, since you don't have to worry about changing the bleed dimensions at some later point.

Bounding Box

The bounding box is the smallest rectangle that can be drawn around all the artwork in the document. It is one of the options you can choose in the Print dialog box or when opening an Illustrator file in Photoshop. The usefulness of the bounding box is debatable since it includes anything on the artboard, including objects that are supposedly masked off, stray points, and unfilled text insertion points. The potential for these elements to unintentionally change the dimensions of the bounding box makes its usage problematic.

Crop Marks

Creating crop marks (Filter > Create > Crop Marks) **A** is a handy way to create quick marks for cropping (duh). You can create as many crop marks as you want in your file, and they are fully editable. What crop marks won't do is actually crop the page for you. They are merely stroked paths.

Crop Area

Setting the crop area is the surest and most versatile way to specify the area of your artwork or design. Just create a rectangle (it must be a perfect rectangle—nothing but right angles allowed) of your final size and while selected choose Object > Crop Area > Make **A**. As long as your crop area is smaller than the artboard, files exported as GIF, JPEG, PDF (see accompanying Insight), and so on will defer to the crop area size. Files opened in Photoshop will open to the crop area size if chosen in the Open dialog.

Remember, you can only have one crop area per file, and they are not selectable. Crop areas can be turned off by selecting Object > Crop Area > Release. ▥

INSIGHT

The Crop Area and PDFs. Using the crop area to define the document size of a PDF has a few advantages. When opening the PDF file in a PDF reader like Acrobat, the file dimensions are defined by the crop area. However, if you reopen the file with Illustrator, your entire art area and all objects (even paths that are outside the crop area) will still be there, just as they were before you closed the file.

Creating a Compound Path

Understanding how compound paths are made and how to make them work for you.

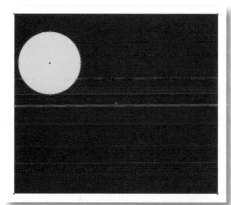

A
Undo Scale
Redo

Group
Join
Average...

Make Clipping Mask
Make Compound Path
Make Guides

Transform ▶
Arrange ▶
Select ▶

1. Create a Compound Path

Using this beautiful piece of artwork by Isabelle Dervaux, we'll do the unthinkable and hide parts of it to show you an example of how you can create a die cut effect with a compound path. Sorry, Isabelle!

Create a new layer above Isabelle's artwork and draw a rectangle on this layer. On top of the new rectangle, draw a circle. Select the rectangle and the circle, and then create a compound path by choosing Object > Compound Path > Make *or* by pressing Cmd (Ctrl)-8 *or* by holding down the Control key (right-clicking) to bring up the contextual menu and choosing Make Compound Path **A**.

2. Duplicate the "Hole"

Using the Direct Selection tool, select the circle (or "hole") and Option (Alt)-Shift-drag to create a copy of the circle. Repeat the transformation by pressing Cmd (Ctrl)-D. Even though there are multiple objects in this compound path, it is still considered a single path or object **A**. The result is a compound path that is easy to move around, and since it's on its own layer, it's easy to hide. 🂠

INSIGHT

What Is a Compound Path? By default, any path or object that is created is "drawn" by Illustrator in a clockwise, or positive, direction **A**. A "hole" is created when you have two overlapping paths and those paths travel in different directions **B**. The "hole" is defined by the path on top. Both paths are then considered a single compound path.

For example, the holes in the letters "O" and "P" are created with compound paths.

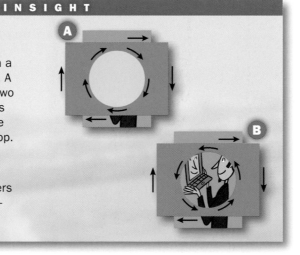

Compound Paths Within Compound Paths

Understanding how compound paths interact with each other by creating a "target" effect.

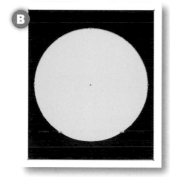

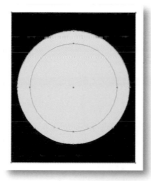

1. Create Concentric Circles

In this example we'll create a "target" effect **A** using a single compound path on top of another piece of artwork by Isabelle. Like the previous example, we created another layer and drew a rectangle with a circle on top of it **B**. Then we created evenly spaced concentric circles 37.5 pt apart (see "Calculation Inside Dialog Boxes and Palettes" in this chapter) by using the Transform palette **C**.

> **T I P**
>
> **Adding to a Compound Path.** It's very easy to add another path to an existing compound path. Just place a new object on top of the compound path, select both objects, and choose Object > Compound Path > Make or press Cmd (Ctrl)-8 (the contextual menu is not available in this instance).

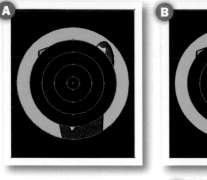

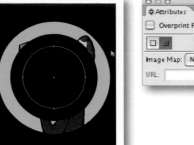

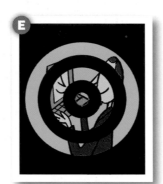

2. Create a Complex Compound Path

Select all the circle objects and create a compound path **A**. Using the Direct Selection tool, select the third circle from the outside, and then go to the Attributes palette and click the Reverse Path Direction Off button **B** (make sure that the Use Non-Zero Winding Fill Rule button **C** is selected). This results in alternating "spaces" being created because each circle is "drawn" in the opposite direction of the circle underneath it. In this case the circle on top is drawn clockwise, whereas the circle underneath is drawn counterclockwise **D**. Reverse the path one last time for the circle in the center **E**.

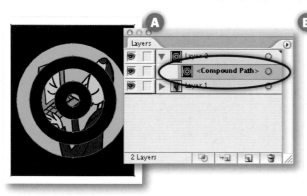

3. Apply a Transparency

Once again, if you select the concentric circles and look at the Layers palette, you'll find that even with all the different objects and the appearance of grouped paths, this is still a single path **A**. Now all we need to do is change the compound path's fill to white and give it an opacity of 40% so that the illustration underneath shows through **B**. As you can see, with a little understanding of compound paths, it's easy to create very complex objects for your projects. ▥

INSIGHT

Stubborn Compound Paths. One of the problems with compound paths is that many times they are made without you knowing it. Using certain pathfinders, outlining text, expanding live trace objects, and more can cause objects to be made that when selected don't seem to want to be filled with a color, grouped with other objects, or joined with other paths. To troubleshoot the problem, you should first suspect that a compound path has been made. If one of your paths is giving you problems, try undoing the compound path by choosing Objects > Compound Path > Release.

Saving and Exporting from Illustrator

For a vector drawing program, Illustrator is extremely flexible when it comes to saving and exporting in various file formats. We recommend that you double-check with your clients or vendors on which format they prefer. For example, many publications, such as newspapers and magazines, will only accept PDF files. Remember to always save a copy of your original artwork as an AI file. That way, you can edit the file in any way, shape, or form without problems if the need arises.

Saving from Illustrator

Illustrator enables you to save your artwork in four native file formats—AI (Adobe Illustrator), PDF (Portable Document Format), EPS (Encapsulated PostScript), and SVG (Scalable Vector Graphic). These formats are able to retain all Illustrator file data so nothing is lost (such as transparency and paths). For PDF and SVG files, be sure to select the Preserve Illustrator Editing Capabilities option when saving. You can also save files as an Illustrator Template file so you can use your saved settings again and again. Here is a short description of each format:

- **AI:** This is Illustrator's truly native file format, which supports any and all features. If you're looking for the best vector file format to import into InDesign, this is it. InDesign will support the AI file format's true, unflattened transparency. If you use other applications, such as Photoshop, AfterEffects, Premiere, GoLive, or Flash, you can't go wrong with the AI file format.

- **PDF:** The PDF format is a ubiquitous file format that embeds both fonts and graphics. This allows you to not have to package fonts and linked images along with your file. Anyone with the free Adobe Acrobat Reader can view your PDF exactly as you see it. What's more, Illustrator is an extremely PDF friendly program. In the PDF Options dialog box, be sure to choose your desired Preset. For example, choose Press Quality if your file is meant for offset printing or Smallest File Size for files that will be viewed on the Web. In addition, be sure to select the Preserve Illustrator Editing Capabilities option if you want to open and fully edit your file in Illustrator. Just be forewarned that this option comes with a price. Your normally highly compressed file will be much larger in size.

- **EPS:** The EPS format is a PostScript file format that can contain either vector or bitmap file data. EPS will retain all of Illustrator's features. You can open and edit EPS files in Illustrator as well as import EPS files into most professional page layout and graphic applications.

C A U T I O N

Illustrator Version Compatibility.
When saving in either AI or EPS formats, be sure to choose your version of Illustrator compatibility in the Illustrator Options box.

- **Illustrator Template:** If you have a file that you want to use repeatedly as a starting point for new files, it makes sense to save that file as a template. This can come in handy for projects such as business cards, flyers, postcards, and so on. Illustrator will not only save the file data, but also any settings, including document setup and print settings, viewing options, color swatches, brushes, graphic styles, symbols, and actions. In addition to the normal Save dialog box, this format is also accessible by choosing File > Save as Template. Also note that when you open a template, Illustrator creates a new document using the template's content and settings, and leaves the original template file unaltered.

- **SVG:** This vector format creates compact, high-quality, interactive graphics used primarily for the Web and mobile devices. You can save your file in two versions: SVG and Compressed SVG. The compressed version squeezes your file size down significantly, but you won't be able to edit the file using a text editor.

Save for Web

In addition to exporting to a Web-appropriate file format, Illustrator also enables you to save a file to those same formats via the Save for Web command. The advantage of using the Save for Web command is that you can better optimize and preview that optimization before saving the file. The Save for Web command allows you to save your file in GIF (Graphics Interchange Format), JPEG (Joint Photographic Experts Group), PNG (Portable Network Graphic), SWF (Flash), SVG (Scalable Vector Graphic), and WBMP (Wireless Bitmap) formats. For details on working with Illustrator graphics and the Web, see Chapter 6.

Save for Microsoft Office

The File > Save for Microsoft Office command lets you save a file that you can use in any Microsoft Office application. The downside is that the only file format it saves in is PNG, and you have no opportunity to customize any settings, such as resolution and transparency. We recommend bypassing this command and using the Export feature, which gives you the ability to specify PNG settings. You also have your choice of other file formats such as TIFF or JPEG, which can be used in Word and PowerPoint, respectively.

Exporting from Illustrator

You can also export artwork in a variety of file formats for use outside of Illustrator. These formats are called non-native formats because Illustrator will not be able to retrieve all of the data if you reopen the file in Illustrator. For this reason, it is recommended that you save your artwork in AI format until you are finished creating it, and then export the artwork to the desired format. The following list provides descriptions of all of the file formats that Illustrator can export via the Export command (File > Export).

- **BMP (bmp):** This format is a common Windows bitmap format. Specify color mode, resolution, and bit-depth for the rasterization process.

- **Targa (tga):** This format is used for graphics that will be displayed using a Truevision video board.

- **PNG (png):** A format for Web graphics, PNG supports 24-bit color and transparency.

- **AutoCAD Drawing (dwg) and AutoCAD Interchange File (dxf):** These two formats are used for saving vector art created in AutoCAD (a computer-aided drafting program) and exchanged between AutoCAD and other programs.

- **Enhanced Metafile (emf):** This is the latest Windows vector file format.

- **GIF (gif):** GIFs are used for spot illustrations and animations on the Web. This format offers good compression for graphics with broad areas of a single color.

- **JPEG (jpg):** JPEG is the format of choice for displaying photographs on the Web and is a format common to many digital cameras. This format offers various quality and compression options.

- **Macintosh PICT (pct):** This format is an old Macintosh file format often used for art that will be output to slides or imported into Microsoft PowerPoint.

- **Photoshop (psd):** The format of choice for exporting Illustrator artwork to Photoshop. For the most part, this format preserves Illustrator layers and text. If it can't, Illustrator preserves the appearance of the art by merging the layers. For detailed information on working between Illustrator and Photoshop, see Chapter 7, "Integrating Illustrator and Photoshop."

- **TIFF (tif):** TIFF is a widely supported, cross-platform bitmap format. It is perfect for importing into page layout and digital imaging applications.

- **Text Format (txt):** This format is used to export Illustrator text to a text file.

- **Windows Metafile (wmf):** This format is a widely supported Windows vector file format. It is an older format that has now been superseded by the newer, and recommended, Enhanced Metafile format. ▥

Working with Adobe Bridge

While Adobe Bridge has its issues, the main complaint being its lack of speed, it has its share of excellent features and productivity enhancers that make up for its less than stellar response time. Adobe Bridge enables you to visually browse, sort, catalogue, and organize all of your digital media assets on your network, and it works with the entire Adobe Creative Suite of applications. You can launch Bridge independently as a standalone application or launch it from Illustrator by choosing File > Browse. Here, we provide you with a road map of the various components that make up Bridge.

Anatomy of Bridge

A *Menu bar:* Commands found on the menu bar allow you to open or delete images, add file information, and search for, view, sort, and tag images. You can also label files and append their metadata. On the Illustrator menu (Tools > Illustrator) you have access to commands such as Live Trace and Export to Flash among others.

B *Look In menu:* This menu lists the folder hierarchy location. Click the up and down arrows to view the particular folder's hierarchy as well as Favorites and Recent Folders. Go back, Go forward, and Go up arrows are also available.

C *Show Filtered/Unfiltered:* This button enables you to restrict image display to rated or labeled files.

D *Shortcut buttons:* With these buttons you can create a new folder, rotate an image 90 degrees clockwise or counterclockwise, and delete files. The last button on the right enables you to switch Bridge to Compact mode.

E *Favorites panel:* This panel provides access to folders as well as Version Cue, Adobe Stock Photos, Collections you've created, and, if you're a Creative Suite user, the Bridge Center. Drag whichever hard drives or folders you want to include in your Favorites panel.

F *Folders panel:* This panel shows the folder hierarchy of all mounted volumes on your computer. To collapse any panel, double-click its tab.

G *Preview panel:* The Preview panel displays the currently selected file. You can reduce or enlarge the preview by dragging the divider lines between the panels.

H *Resize panels/Content window:* Drag the bar that divides the panels from the Content window. Position your cursor over the bar and click and drag to size.

I *Content window:* The largest area of the Content window displays your assets. This window shows thumbnail images of all the files along with information, such as filename and last modified date, in the currently selected folder. In addition, any subfolders are shown with a folder icon.

J *Keywords panel:* This panel lets you tag your images with keywords, such as the names of people or places, enabling you to more easily locate and sort images.

K *Metadata panel:* This data-packed panel shows information about your images. The File Properties section shows items such as filename, date of creation, date last modified, image format, size, and so on. File information, such as the name, address, and email address of the creator of the file, is displayed in the IPTC section of the Metadata palette. The Camera Data section displays information associated with your digital photos, such as the make and model of your camera, exposure, and ISO speed. You can also display other types of metadata by choosing them in the Preferences dialog box accessed via the Metadata palette pop-up menu.

L *Show/Hide Panels:* This left/right arrow button displays all components or only the Content window.

M *Viewing controls:* The thumbnail slider enables you to reduce or enlarge the display of file thumbnails. The remaining four buttons change the view from thumbnails to filmstrip, to details, and to versions and alternates (for Version Cue users). 🁢

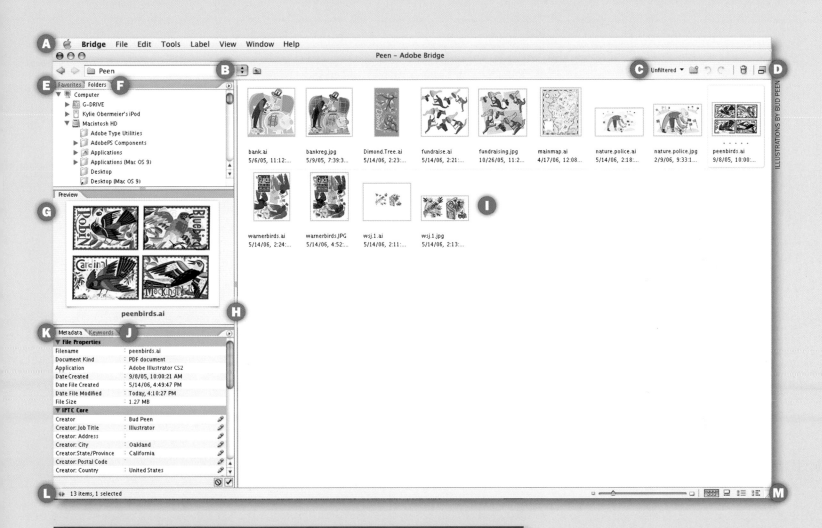

ILLUSTRATIONS BY BUD PEEN

Bridge Features

Now that you've had an anatomical lesson of Bridge's many components, here is a short description of some of its main features.

File Browsing

ILLUSTRATIONS BY BUD PEEN

One of the primary features of Bridge is its use as a navigation tool. You can visually browse through volumes and folders to quickly find your desired file. Use the Folders panel to expand or collapse folders in the folder tree hierarchy. You can also quickly find your frequently accessed folders if you add them to your Favorites panel. Simply drag the folder into the Favorites list. Once you've located the file, select it and you're rewarded with a high-quality, scalable preview. Make your preview smaller or larger by adjusting the divider line between the panels. Note that you can use the Filmstrip view mode to get a large preview without any resizing. Use the various commands on the *File* menu to open the file. You can double-click or choose File > Open, or you can choose File > Open With to open the file in its native application. You can also delete files by selecting them and simply pressing the Delete key or by choosing File >

Move to Trash. Add or remove folders from your Favorites panel by choosing File > Add to Favorites or Remove from Favorites.

On the *Edit* menu, you'll find commands that enable you to select files (all files, those currently not selected, labeled, or unlabeled) and cut, copy, paste, and duplicate them. The Find command is a powerful browsing feature on the Edit menu that enables you to find files in selected folders based on a variety of criteria, such as filename, date, labels, or keywords. Once you have executed a search, you can then click the Save As Collection button at the top of the Content window. You can then later search based on that Collection name in the Favorites panel.

The options on the *View* menu allow you to selectively choose how you want to view your files—in a slide show format, as thumbnails (the default), a filmstrip, details, or versions and alternates

File Management

(Version Cue). Note that your thumbnail size can be changed via the slider at the bottom right of the Content window. You can also sort your files by criteria such as name and date, or labels and ratings (described in the following "File Management" section). You can also show just vector files, which can help separate your illustrations from your photos. Finally, you can display and hide your various panels by toggling them on and off.

In addition to seeing a large preview of your selected image, you can also view the *metadata* information that is embedded in your image file. The metadata categories include the following defaults:

- **File Properties:** In this category you'll find items such as filename, size, format, color mode, and so on.

- **IPTC (International Press Telecommunications Council):** This category covers items used by the media, and includes data such as credit lines, sources, headlines, description, copyright, and usage rights, among many others.

- **Camera Data (EXIF or Extended File Information):** EXIF data is information attached to an image created from a digital camera, such as make and model of the camera, exposure, and f-stop settings. If a digital camera didn't capture the image, it doesn't have any EXIF data, although some scanners attach EXIF data, such as date, time, pixel dimensions, and resolution.

Note that you can enter the metadata directly in the panel or choose File > File Info to add certain metadata.

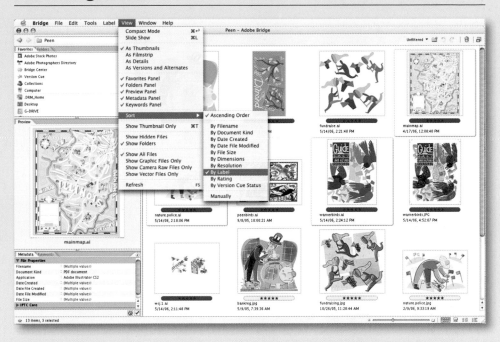

With Bridge, you can *rate and label* your files. This allows you to later sort and then view your files according to their designated rating (based on 1–5 stars) or label (based on colors). Simply select your images and on the Label menu choose your desired star rating or color label. Use the Sort menu (View > Sort) or the Show Filtered/Unfiltered drop-down menu at the top left of the Bridge window to choose your desired criteria. Those files then display in the Content window.

With the use of *keywords*, Bridge offers yet another way for you to tag and then later sort and view your images. Keywords are descriptive labels that you attach to files. They help to categorize your images, enabling you to more efficiently locate your files. Click the folder icon at the bottom of the Keywords panel to create a keyword set. Name your set. Click the New keyword icon (dog-eared page) and enter your desired keyword. To apply a keyword, select your desired files and select the box to the left of the keyword. To search for keywords, choose Find from the Keywords panel pop-up menu. Choose your desired folder from the Look In menu or click Browse to navigate to your folder. Select your search criteria and click Search. All images tagged with your keyword will appear in the Content window.

Bridge Center

Color Management

If you have Creative Suite 2 installed, you also have access to the Bridge Center (found in your Favorites panel), where you can read news, get tips about Adobe applications, view your recently used folders and files, and access Adobe Stock Photos (also available directly in your Favorites panel). You can also save file groups (sets of files you want saved as a group, even from separate applications).

You can use Bridge to synchronize the color settings across all your Creative Suite applications to ensure color accuracy and consistency. Choose Edit > Creative Suite Color Settings and select Show Expanded List of Color Settings. Choose your desired predefined color setting and click Apply. For more details, see the "Color Management" section later in this chapter.

Other Bridge Features

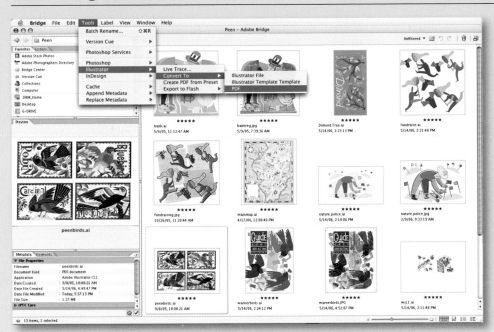

*****
fundraise.ai
5/14/06, 2:21:48 PM

*****
nature.police.jpg
2/9/06, 9:33:19 AM

Here are a few other features that Bridge supports:

- **Additional tools:** On the Illustrator menu (Tools > Illustrator) you'll find four commands. Select a file, or multiple files, and then choose commands such as Live Trace, Convert To, Create PDF from Preset, or Export to Flash. All of these commands or functions are also found in Illustrator and are explained in detail in other sections in this book.

- **Camera Raw capability:** Although you may not find the need in Illustrator, Bridge can also open and edit Camera Raw files (File > Open in Camera File) and save them in a Photoshop compatible file format.

- **Version Cue support:** If you have Creative Suite 2 installed, you can use Bridge to manage your Version Cue projects. Version Cue helps you organize and manage versions of your files as you (and others if you're in a collaborative work environment) work on them.

Color Management

An essential component to any Illustrator workflow is being able to utilize some color management. How far you want to take it is up to you, but at a minimum you'll want to calibrate your monitor and establish your color settings and profiles.

CAUTION

Testing Is the Key. Remember, color management is more an art than a science. Unfortunately, we don't truly live in a 100% WYSIWYG world. Learning all you can about color management and spending some time testing and experimenting with your own personal workflow and equipment will give you the best approximation from screen to paper, screen to another screen, or screen to other forms of output.

Get Ready

Establish an optimum environment for viewing your images by following a few guidelines:

- Keep the lighting (the level, intensity, and temperature) in your work area as consistent as possible. View your onscreen images and your prints under the same lighting, so you can establish a benchmark to use for any necessary color adjustments.

- Keep the walls surrounding your monitor as neutral as possible.

- Keep your computer desktop a neutral gray. Desktop colors and patterns will influence how you view your images.

- For print work, use a color swatch book (Pantone, Trumatch, or the ink company of your choice) to choose your colors. Be sure to also use a swatch book for your chosen paper type—coated or uncoated. Color swatch books are a more accurate way to spec color for offset printing.

- If you are outsourcing your printing, find a vendor you like and trust, and then stick with that vendor. After awhile, you'll know what to expect and again will be able to establish a benchmark for any necessary color tweaks.

Calibrate Your Monitor

By calibrating your monitor you will remove any color casts and make your monitor as neutral as possible. You will also create a profile that tells your operating system how your monitor is displaying color. The best way to calibrate your monitor is to use a combination software and hardware calibration system that includes a device called a colorimeter (www.colorvision.com). For a low budget (and lower accuracy) option, if you're using Windows, calibrate your monitor using the Adobe Gamma utility, which is found in the Control Panel folder. If you're using Mac OS X, use the Display Calibrator Assistant. Choose Apple > System Preferences > Displays > Color and then click Calibrate. Let your monitor warm up a good 30 minutes before running the utility. Color experts advise you to calibrate weekly or, at a minimum, monthly.

TIP

Switching Color Modes. When you first create a document in Illustrator, you're asked to specify either an RGB or CMYK color mode. If you change your mind after the fact, it's not a problem. Simply choose File > Document Color Mode and switch to your desired mode.

Specify Your Color Settings

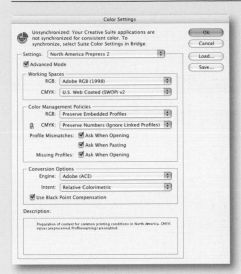

Next you'll want to establish your desired color settings to ensure that they will be optimum for your type of output. In Illustrator, choose Edit > Color Settings. In the Color Settings dialog box you can choose from predefined settings or customize your own configuration to fit your needs.

If you want to go the predefined route, choose one of the presets from the Settings pop-up menu. Once selected, Illustrator will provide all the appropriate working spaces and conversion policies. If your chosen preset describes your workflow, you can feel comfortable (with an exception—see "Caution: Other Color Settings") that the predefined setting will provide you with good results. Be sure to

select Advanced Mode to access the full array of presets. Note that you can switch freely from one preset to another. For example, use North America Prepress 2 when preparing images for print, and then switch to North America Web/Internet when working with files for the Web. You can also use a preset as a starting point and then adjust any individual settings. When you do so, your setting name will default to Custom.

Assign Your Working Spaces

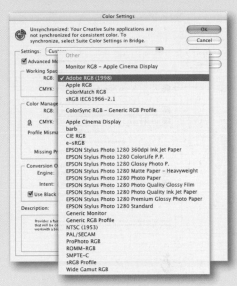

By choosing a preset from the Settings menu, specific color profiles are automatically assigned to your RGB and CMYK working spaces. For example, Prepress 2 uses Adobe RGB (1998) as the RGB working space, which is optimum for converting files to CMYK for printing. The CMYK working space is US Web Coated, which is the standard for offset printing in North America. Note that your offset printing company may supply you with a custom CMYK setting, which you'll want to load.

Every file you create on your computer will use the colors within the gamut of your chosen color profiles. Keep in mind that even if you chose a preset setting, you can choose a different working space if necessary. Your setting will then default to Custom. When you save your file, be sure to check the Embed ICC Profiles option in the Illustrator Options dialog box. This will ensure that the file will be embedded with that color profile, and the working space in which it was created will always be known.

Specifying Color Management Policies

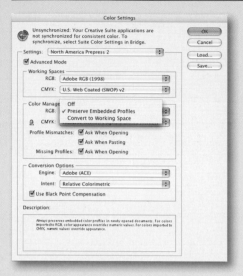

You will also need to specify how Illustrator manages the color profiles of the files it opens. Illustrator needs to know what to do when it encounters a *Profile Mismatch*—that is, when it opens a file that has an embedded color profile that doesn't match your particular working space. Note that you may also encounter a *Missing Profile*—files that have no embedded profile. These files were either created in the pre-color-managed days, with color management turned off, or from an application that doesn't support color management. With Missing Profile files, you'll want to assign your particular working space.

To manage the mismatch encounter, you have three options:

- *Off:* Illustrator doesn't utilize any color management when opening files.

- *Preserve Embedded Profiles:* Illustrator will display the file in its embedded color space and will not perform any color conversions.

- *Convert to Working Space:* Illustrator will convert the file from its embedded color space to your working color space.

With CMYK images you have an additional option:

- *Preserve Numbers (Ignore Linked Profiles):* Illustrator will ignore all embedded profiles, but will preserve the color numbers in the file and still allow you to use color management. This is the recommended option if you want to work in what is termed a "safe" CMYK workflow—your color numbers are preserved throughout the printing process.

Be cautious about allowing for CMYK conversions. If you get a Profile Mismatch with a CMYK image, you will most likely want to preserve the image's embedded profile unless you know for sure that it should be converted to another CMYK working space.

We recommend selecting the Ask When Opening and Ask When Pasting options. This way you'll be alerted when there is a profile mismatch, and you'll have the choice of preserving or converting on a file by file basis. Otherwise, Illustrator automatically follows your color management policies without an alert. This is especially important if, for example, you prepare graphics for print and Web; you'll want to decide whether you want to leave the embedded profile or convert depending on what the intended output is for the file. Note that when you choose the Advanced Mode option, you'll have more options regarding color conversion engines and rendering intents (color translation methods). Leave these options at their defaults unless you are well versed in color management.

Viewing a Proof

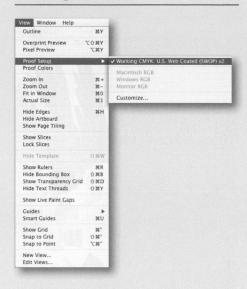

Printing with Color Management

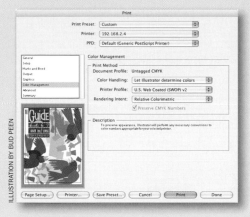

ILLUSTRATION BY BUD PEEN

Synchronizing Color Across All CS2 Applications

Illustrator also enables you to preview how your file will look in different color spaces or on different output devices without actually making any changes to the physical file. Choose View > Proof Setup and select your device. Here are your available options:

- **Working CMYK** is based on the CMYK setting you chose in the Color Settings dialog box.

- **Macintosh RGB/Windows RGB** displays your file as it would appear on a generic Mac or PC. This is handy for previewing Web graphics.

- **Monitor RGB** uses your monitor's color profile, thereby ignoring any Adobe color management.

- **Customize** enables you to choose from a variety of color spaces and devices, including all of the working spaces found in the Color Settings dialog box, various video formats, and printers.

After you've chosen your desired setup, choose View > Proof Colors to view the image in that space.

Nothing can replace good, old-fashioned experimentation when it comes to getting the color you want output on paper. Some experts say to let your printer, especially if it is a high-end device, determine the color. Others say to leave the color management to Illustrator. But if you need a starting point, you can follow these suggestions.

Choose File > Print. Choose Color Management from the left column. For Color Handling, choose Let Illustrator Determine Colors. For Printer Profile, choose your particular printer's profile. Leave Rendering Intent set to Relative Colorimetric. If you are printing a CMYK file, leave the Preserve CMYK Numbers option selected. If your print isn't satisfactory, try changing the Color Handling setting to Let PostScript Printer Determine Colors. If you're still not happy, experiment by trying different printer profiles.

When all of your CS2 applications are using the same color settings, your color management is said to be synchronized and will be annotated as such at the top of your Color Settings dialog box. Most of the time this is a good thing because it will get you closer to consistent color across all applications. Note that you may want to have different color settings in applications such as InDesign (print) and GoLive (Web). This is perfectly acceptable.

By using Adobe Bridge to set up your color management, your settings are automatically synchronized. In Illustrator, choose File > Browse or launch Bridge directly. Choose Edit > Creative Suite Color Settings. Select Show Expanded List of Color Settings Files. Choose your desired predefined color setting and click Apply. Consider yourself synchronized. You can choose a previously saved custom setting as well. ▦

2

FREEFORM DRAWING AND GEOMETRIC SHAPES

Basic Drawing and Beyond

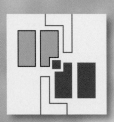

DESPITE ALL THE BELLS and whistles Illustrator has garnered over its lifetime, its heart and soul lie with its capability to create pure vector graphics—from a simple circle to a more exotic perfect spiral. But why is it that sometimes the simplest things to create often require the most skill or practice? We'll start with that valuable asset, the Pathfinder palette. Next, we'll move on to the nitty-gritty basics of drawing with the Pen tool, and then end with the powerful but more involved features of the Appearance palette, Live Paint, and Live Trace.

Perfecting the Pen

This chapter gives you some pointers on becoming a proficient user of Illustrator's primary drawing tool—the Pen. Used for everything from drawing illustrations to creating custom typography to plucking objects out of raster images by creating a masking path, the Pen tool is without a doubt the workhorse of the Illustrator Tools palette. Although it is sometimes obstinate and unruly, once you've got it down, you'll definitely reap the rewards of its capabilities. And as an added bonus, you'll find the same tool in Photoshop and InDesign.

Pathfinder and Drawing Strategies

But don't get us wrong; sometimes there are easier ways to create the object you want than by drawing it freehand with the Pen tool. That's where the almighty Pathfinder palette comes to the rescue. By enabling you to add to, subtract from, trim, and divide paths, the Pathfinder palette can save you a tremendous amount of "manual labor," leaving you time for the finessing. After you've learned the practicalities, we'll provide

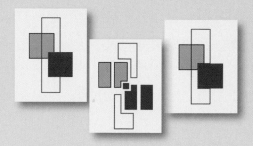

some food for thought on how to rethink the way you approach a drawing. Rather than thinking of an illustration as a single object, we'll show you the benefits of thinking of it as a series of overlapping segments. This enables you to more easily make those inevitable edits to your illustrations.

Select Same and Select Object Time-Savers

Once you have the skeleton of a drawing, you often have to make selections to change colors, alter stroke weights, find masks, and so on. In a fairly complex drawing it doesn't take long to realize that having to manually pick through the multiple stacks and numerous layers to find all the objects you want is extremely time-consuming. Using the Select > Same and Select > Object menus enables you to quickly find objects based on similar fills, strokes, weight, opacity, and so on. After you've made a selection, you can save it for future use. When you become accustomed to using the menu commands, you'll never again manually dissect your illustration to make selections.

Symbols, Styles, and the Appearance Palette

If you just skimmed the surface of Illustrator's basic features, you may have overlooked goodies such as Symbols, Graphic Styles, and the Appearance palette. The first two features can be real productivity boosters, enabling you to create an object or style once and then use it again and again. The Appearance palette enables you to apply attributes to your objects without actually altering its underlying structure. A single object can have multiple fills and strokes, all with different colors, weights, opacities, and effects. And if you encounter a problem with your object, you'll probably find the solution in the Appearance palette.

Live Paint and Trace

We round out the chapter by introducing you to two new features in Illustrator CS2. While by no means mandatory features that must be mastered, Live Paint and Live Trace are features that can certainly make your digital illustrating more efficient and even fun. If you want a more intuitive way to create a drawing while retaining a lot of editing flexibility, be sure to check out the section "Non-Destructive Color Panes with Live Paint." If you need to trace a scanned sketch or photograph, Live Trace can be a lifesaver in what would otherwise be a tedious and lengthy project.

Enough introductions. Let's dive in!

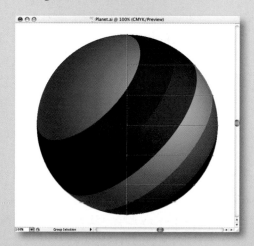

Pathfinder Revealed

The Pathfinder palette is one of the most useful and powerful features in Illustrator. Following are examples of what Shape Modes and Pathfinders can do and how the stacking order and strokes of the objects affect them.

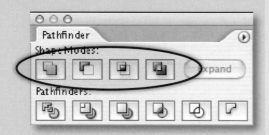

SHAPE MODES

Illustrator has four Shape Modes: Add, Subtract, Intersect, and Exclude.

Add

The Add Shape Mode combines selected paths into a compound shape and gives the appearance of a single object. If expanded, the objects become a single path or a compound path if the result has a "hole."

Attributes: The resulting object takes on the characteristics of the topmost object selected.

Strokes: Retained only if specified in the topmost object.

Note: This is probably the most popular of all the Shape Modes.

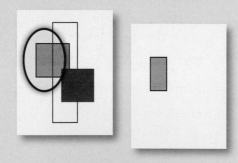

Subtract

The Subtract Shape Mode combines selected paths into a compound shape and gives the appearance of all shapes being "knocked out" of the bottommost object. If expanded, the result is a single path.

Attributes: The resulting object takes on the characteristics of the bottommost object selected.

Strokes: Retained only if specified in the bottommost object.

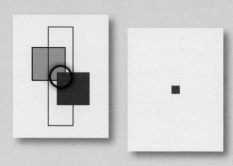

Intersect

The Intersect Shape Mode combines selected paths into a compound shape and gives the appearance of showing only the areas where the objects overlap. If expanded, the result is a single path.

Attributes: The resulting object takes on the characteristics of the topmost object selected.

Strokes: Retained only if specified in the topmost object.

Note: All objects selected must have a common overlap, or, if they don't have a common overlap, the objects must be part of a group that has a common overlap.

Exclude

The Exclude Shape Mode combines selected paths into a compound shape and gives the appearance of "knocking out" the shapes where the objects overlap. If expanded, the objects become a single path or a compound path if the result has a "hole."

Attributes: The resulting object takes on the characteristics of the topmost object selected.

Strokes: Retained only if specified in the topmost object.

Note: For many, this might be an easier way to create compound paths (see Chapter 1, "Program Foundations"), because you can continually use the Exclude button to add to the shape.

PATHFINDERS

Illustrator has six Pathfinders: Divide, Trim, Merge, Crop, Outline, and Minus Back.

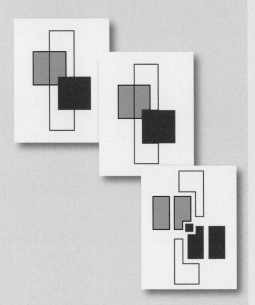

Divide

The most productive and well-used Pathfinder, Divide slices objects based on overlapping paths, *not* on appearance.

Attributes: The resulting objects take on the characteristics of the topmost objects in the stacking order.

Strokes: Inconsistent; there are so many caveats for strokes using the Divide Pathfinder that it would take another chapter to explain them.

Note: Since this Pathfinder divides all paths whether or not they are visible, it is not the best choice if you want to avoid creating unfilled/unstroked paths. Also, you might consider using Live Paint (see "Non-Destructive Color Panes with Live Paint" later in this chapter) instead of the Divide Pathfinder since it will give you greater editing flexibility.

Trim

The Trim Pathfinder removes all overlapping areas based on their appearance, *not* on the actual paths.

Attributes: The resulting objects take on the fill characteristics of the topmost objects in the stacking order.

Strokes: The Trim Pathfinder *is incompatible with strokes*. Outline all strokes before using this tool, or in the case of a stroke with no fill, you will end up deleting the path. Objects with a fill *and* a stroke will lose the stroke attribute.

Note: The Trim Pathfinder comes in very handy for exporting finished artwork to Flash. One of the most often used features in Flash is the ability to fade or overlap a symbol using an alpha Color Style. Unfortunately, if artwork is made up of overlapping shapes, each shape will show through the other. Using the Trim Pathfinder eliminates the overlap, and when exported to Flash, makes for a cleaner alpha effect.

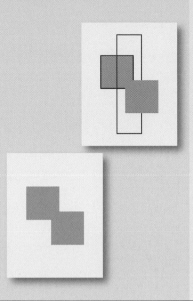

Merge

The Merge Pathfinder works essentially the same as the Trim Pathfinder with one notable exception—overlapping paths with the same fill color will be united into a single path.

Attributes: The resulting objects take on the fill characteristics of the topmost objects in the stacking order.

Strokes: The Merge Pathfinder is incompatible with strokes. Outline all strokes before using this tool, or in the case of a stroke with no fill, you will end up deleting the path. Objects with a fill and a stroke will lose the stroke attribute.

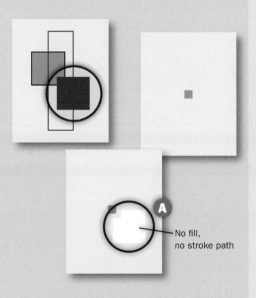

No fill,
no stroke path

Crop

The Crop Pathfinder removes any areas and objects that fall outside the topmost object's shape.

Attributes: The resulting objects take on the characteristics of the topmost objects in the stacking order (but are beneath the initial object that is the basis of the crop) and also can create unfilled and unstroked paths in areas that are empty **A** (empty area is shown in white).

Strokes: Like the Trim and Merge Pathfinders, Crop is incompatible with strokes.

Note: The Crop Pathfinder does not affect placed raster images.

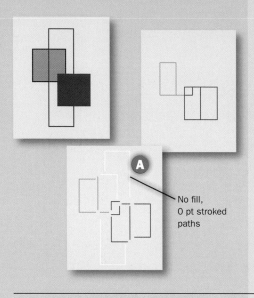

No fill,
0 pt stroked
paths

Outline

The Outline Pathfinder converts all paths to strokes and at the same time divides the paths where they intersect.

Attributes: The resulting objects take on the stroke characteristics of the topmost objects in the stacking order.

Strokes: Any object that had a fill and no stroke converts to a no-fill 0 pt stroke (a 0 pt stroke is shown in white **A**).

Note: There are very few times when you would use this Pathfinder since the result is extremely severe.

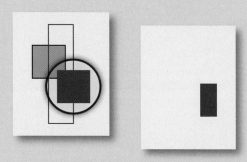

Minus Back

The Minus Back Pathfinder, a holdover from the original Pathfinder filters, removes any selected areas from the topmost object. The basic functionality is the same as the Subtract Shape Mode (though reversed) except the result is instantaneous.

Attributes: The resulting object takes on the characteristics of the topmost object selected.

Strokes: Retained only if specified in the topmost object.

Note: Why this is a Pathfinder and not a Shape Mode is anyone's guess. ▦

Becoming a Pen Master

While not the most user-friendly tool in the shed, the Pen tool is definitely one of the sharpest.

Most artists love the Pencil tool. It's fun, friendly, and a cinch to use. It works like its analog alter ego. Press and drag to create a path that mimics the movement of your hand. Add a stylus and drawing tablet and who the heck needs paper? However, the Pen tool, whose deceiving little icon looks like the tip of a fountain pen, doesn't come close to working like its analog version. Press and drag and you're presented with alien antennae that shoot out from either side of a point. Welcome to the world of Bézier curves. While the Pen's methodology may take some getting used to, its precision and control is nothing to turn up your nose at. In this section, we'll offer some tips that will enable you to wield the Pen with ease.

Anatomy of a Path

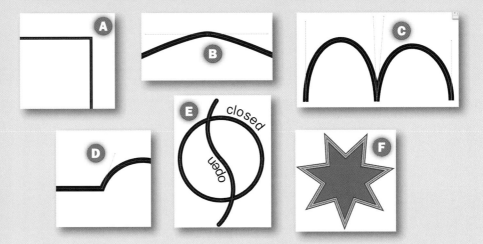

Even though most Illustrator users are quite familiar with paths, we'll just offer a short review of some of their major components. Having a detailed understanding of each component can help you create your paths more accurately and more quickly.

- *Paths are comprised of three components: anchor points (corner, smooth, and cusp), straight segments, and curved segments.* The combination of these three components creates straight and curved paths. Curved segments get additional assistance from direction lines (described in the following items).

- *A corner point* has no direction lines. Corner points are used for shapes such as stars and buildings **A**.

- *A smooth point* has two direction lines pointing (nonprinting) in opposite directions. The direction lines are tangential to the curve. Moving one of the lines also moves the other in the exact opposite direction. Smooth points are used to draw everything that isn't perfectly angular **B**.

- *A cusp point* has two direction lines that are independent of one another. Use cusp points when drawing objects with curves going in the same direction, such as petals on a flower **C**.

- *A point between a straight segment and a curved segment* is a corner point with only one direction line **D**.

- *A path can be open or closed*, such as in a square or circle. You can close an open path or open a closed path. To find out how, check out the section, "Editing Paths" **E**.

- *A path can have a stroke, a fill, or both.* In fact, a path can have multiple fills and strokes if you use the Appearance palette **F**.

- *When you deselect your paths*, you will not see your anchor points or direction lines. To see direction lines, select the corresponding anchor point with the Direct Selection tool. Selected anchor points are filled; unselected anchor points are hollow.

Creating Straight Paths

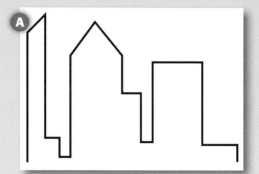

Creating straight paths is one of the easiest tasks to accomplish in Illustrator. Simply select the Pen tool and click and release your mouse button at the points where you want the line to begin and end. Continue to click, and your Pen will continue to create straight segments connected to your anchor points **A**. To constrain your path—horizontally, vertically, or at any 45 degree angle—hold down the Shift key as you click. To end the path and leave it as an open path, click the Pen tool in the Tools palette to deselect the path. Or better yet, press the Cmd (Ctrl) key, which gives you your last used Selection tool, and click anywhere away from the path. Release the Cmd (Ctrl) key and you're back to your Pen tool.

T I P

The Straight Scoop. You can also create straight segments with the Line Segment tool. Press and drag to create a straight segment with two end anchor points. Or click and release on your artboard to bring up the Line Segment Tool Options dialog box where you can enter the length and angle of your line.

T I P

Paths Make the Mask. You can use any path, straight or curved, as a masking element for both raster and vector art. For more on masks, see Chapter 3 "Masks and Blend Effects."

PHOTOSPIN

T I P

Draw with None. When using the Pen to create artwork in the Preview mode, it's best to set your Fill to None. If you don't, your path will keep filling with color as you draw, making it hard to see what you're doing at times. Remember, Illustrator fills open paths as well as closed paths. With open paths, Illustrator simply finds the shortest route between the two open end points and creates a boundary for the fill.

T I P

Leave Vector Creation to Illustrator. Since Illustrator is a superior program when it comes to creating vector paths, you might want to create them in Illustrator even if their final destination is Photoshop. To export your paths to Photoshop, check out Chapter 7, "Integrating Illustrator and Photoshop."

Creating Curved Paths

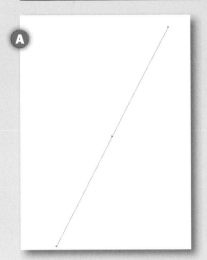

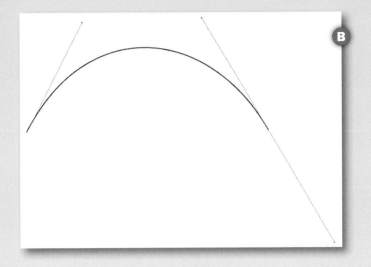

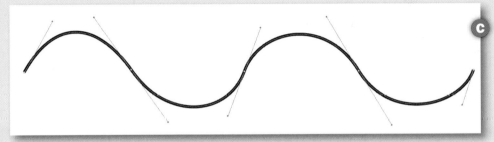

Curved paths are referred to as Bézier curves. They get their exotic moniker from Pierre Bézier, a mathematician who in the 1970s invented the equation used for CAD/CAM programs. Yes, the beautiful curves that create your organic shapes are actually based on a mathematical cubic equation where the path is controlled by direction lines that end in direction points. The length and angle of the direction lines control the appearance of the curve.

Here are some steps and tips for creating the curve you require:

1. With the Pen tool, position your cursor where you want the curve to begin. Drag toward the direction that you want the arc

of the curve to go. How far should you drag? Use what we call the "one third rule." Visualize the curve you want to draw and divide it into thirds. Then drag your mouse approximately the length of one third. Drag straight up from the anchor point for a steeper curve or drag at an angle from the anchor point for a flatter curve.

2. Release the mouse button. You'll see the appearance of an anchor point with two direction lines, which have direction points at the ends **A**. Remember, the direction lines/points control the angle and pitch of the curve.

3. Move the cursor to the position where you want the curve to end and drag in

the opposite direction, away from the arc. You'll see another anchor point and a set of direction lines/points. Illustrator creates the curve segment between the points **B**. If you drag in the same direction, you create an "S" shaped curve instead of an arc shaped curve.

It's important to try to keep the anchor points on either side of the curve, not along the top. It is also wise to use the fewest number of anchor points possible to create your path. The result will be a smoother curve, a smaller file size, and a reduction in potential printing snafus.

4. To draw more curves that alternate in direction, repeat steps 1–3 **C**.

Connecting Paths

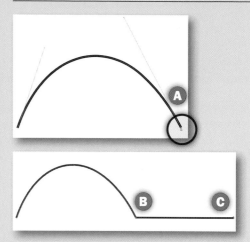

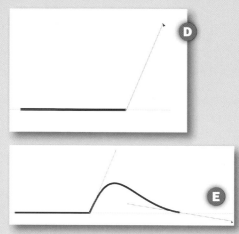

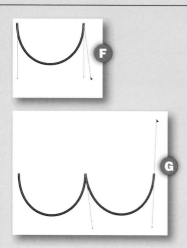

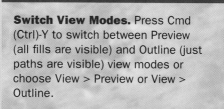

To continue adding to a previously open path, make sure you position your cursor on the last anchor point you created on that open path. A slash mark or small square will appear next to your cursor. Click on that anchor point to continue drawing the path.

If you are adding a straight segment to a curve, you'll need to convert the point where the path changes from curved to straight. Here's how:

1. To convert a point, position your Pen cursor over the end smooth anchor point. A caret symbol appears next to the Pen icon **A**. Click and release your mouse over the anchor point. The bottom direction line disappears. The smooth point has now been converted into a corner point with one direction line **B**.

2. Move your Pen cursor to where you want your straight segment to end and click and release. If you want to constrain the line horizontally, vertically, or at an angle of 45 degrees, hold down the Shift key as you click. Illustrator creates your straight segment **C**.

If you are adding a curve to a straight segment, you'll also need to convert the point where the path changes from straight to curved. The steps are similar:

1. To convert the point so that a curve can be added, position your Pen cursor over the end corner point (again you'll see the caret) and drag. As you drag you'll create a direction line from the anchor point **D**. Drag your desired angle and distance. A pure corner point has now been converted into a corner point with one direction line.

2. Move your Pen cursor to where you want your curve segment to end and drag. Illustrator creates your curve segment **E**.

If you want to connect curves that arc in the same direction, you'll need to create cusp points in between. Follow these steps:

1. To convert the point so that another curve with the same arc direction can be added, position your Pen cursor over the end smooth point. Press the Option (Alt) key and click and release over the point. The bottom direction line disappears.

2. Keep your Pen cursor over the anchor point and drag in the direction of the arc of your curve at your desired angle and distance. Release your mouse. As you drag you'll create a direction line from the anchor point. Now you have two direction lines on the same side of the anchor point, yet both are independent of one another **F**. You've created a cusp point.

3. Position your Pen cursor where you want the curve to end and drag in the opposite direction as step 2. You should now have a second curve arcing in the same direction as the first **G**.

T I P

Switch View Modes. Press Cmd (Ctrl)-Y to switch between Preview (all fills are visible) and Outline (just paths are visible) view modes or choose View > Preview or View > Outline.

Closing and Opening Paths

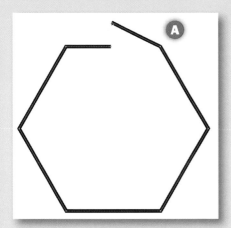

To close any path, simply return to your starting anchor point and click. A small circle appears next to your Pen cursor, alerting you that you're closing the path.

To open a closed path, grab the Scissors tool and position it where you want to open, or cut, the path, and then click and release. If you're cutting on a curve, the Scissors tool creates two smooth points on each end of the opening. If you're cutting a straight segment, it creates two corner points. To see the actual opening, first deselect the object. Then with your Direct Selection tool, select one of the newly created anchor points and drag it away from the path **A**.

Editing Paths

Usually, it is easier and quicker to get a good but not absolutely perfect path to represent what it is you're trying to draw. Then you can fine-tune the path by manipulating the anchor points, the direction lines, and segments. Illustrator offers several editing tools that make your path refinements possible. Here is a rundown on how to edit your paths:

• The *Add Anchor Point tool and Delete Anchor Point tool* add and delete anchor points within your path. If you deselect the Disable Auto Add/Delete preference (Illustrator > Preferences > General), you can use the Pen tool to add and delete anchor points. Simply position your Pen cursor where you want to add a point (you'll see a plus sign next to the cursor) on the path and click and release. To delete a point, position your Pen cursor over it (you'll see a minus sign) and click and release.

• The *Convert Point tool* changes a smooth point to a corner point and *vice versa.* To change a smooth point to a corner, position your Pen cursor over it (you'll see a caret sign) and click and release **A**. To convert a corner to a smooth point, position your Pen cursor over it and click and drag to create your direction lines. To convert a smooth point to a cusp point, make sure the direction lines are showing and then

drag a direction line to break it into independent direction lines. And to convert a cusp point back to a smooth point, drag out from the anchor point.

• The *Direct Selection tool* enables you to select components of the path separately. If you need to reposition an anchor point or lengthen or change the angle of a direction line, grab this popular tool, select your component, and drag. Remember, by lengthening or shortening the direction line you can control how steep or flat the curve is. By rotating the direction line, you change the slope of the curve.

• You can also use the *Transform tools* (Scale, Rotate, Skew, and Reflect) on any path, open or closed.

• Use the *Reshape tool* to alter the shape of a segment of your path. If your path is slightly more jagged than you want, use the *Smooth tool* and drag over the jagged segment to smooth it out.

• Grab the *Eraser tool* and drag along a portion of your path to delete it. Try to use a single, smooth "tracing" motion for the best results.

• To cut an object consisting of a closed path, such as a polygon or freeform shape, into two separate objects, each with closed paths, select the *Knife tool* and drag through the object. ▥

Drawing Strategies

The best way to draw an object is not necessarily to go from point A to point B. Here are some tips for creating artwork faster and with more flexibility.

Drawing with Shapes

Sometimes, rather than using the Pen tool to draw your element freehand, it's easier to start with a simple shape, such as a circle or square, and modify the paths to create a more complex shape as we did with a clover and flower. We used the Add Anchor Point and Convert Point tools to create the clover **A**. For the flower, we started with a circle and used the Add Anchor Point command (Object > Add Anchor Point) a few times. Then we added the Bloat effect and, *voilà!*—a perfectly symmetrical flower in under 3 seconds.

Additionally, you can draw a few simple shapes and use the awesome Pathfinder palette to then combine your shapes into a single path, which is what we did with the cloud **B**. For more on the Pathfinder palette, see the earlier section "Pathfinder Revealed."

Drawing with Overlapping Segments

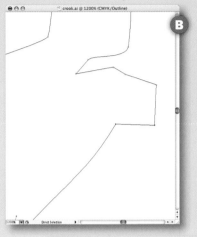

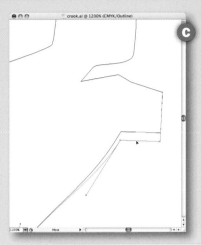

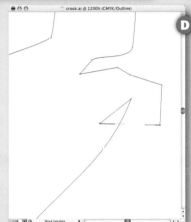

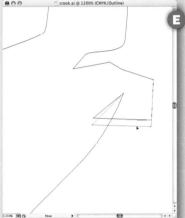

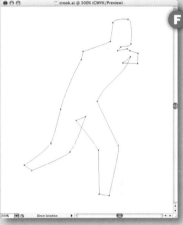

When creating an illustration or design, you would normally use the Pen tool and draw point to point. However, in some instances it's preferable to think of your artwork as a series of path segments rather than a single object. In this example, a figure is drawn in normal point-to-point fashion **A**. The curve of the body is exactly the way we want it to be **B**, but if we try to change the arm, the curve of the body is altered too **C**. If we think of the arm and the curve of the body as separate path segments and draw them so that the segments overlap but don't connect at any particular anchor point **D**, we can then move or modify the arm independently of the body curve **E**. Even though the segments overlap, how the artwork previews and prints is exactly the same **F**.

Using Overlapping Segments with a Pathfinder or Live Paint

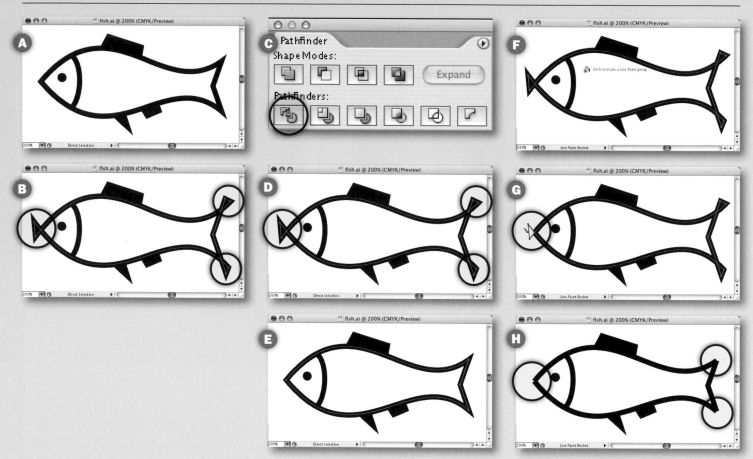

The creation of this artwork **A** is along the same lines as the previous example but with a twist. Instead of an inner corner where the segments overlap, these segments overlap at the outer corner, necessitating the deletion of the excess paths **B**. There are two ways to accomplish this.

One option is to use the Divide Pathfinder **C** (see "Pathfinder Revealed" earlier in this chapter) to divide the path at the intersection **D**, and then delete the excess path **E**. The obvious disadvantage to using the Divide Pathfinder is that after you apply it, it's harder to modify the object later.

The other option is to use Live Paint (see "Non-Destructive Color Panes with Live Paint" later in this chapter) **F** and stroke the excess path with None **G**. This preserves the editability of the object, but since there is a stroke involved, using Live Paint is not an option because of its inability to correctly interpret the intersections of the object **H**. However, if this were a filled object instead of a stroked object, the Live Paint option would work.

Transform Tool Shortcuts

ILLUSTRATION BY TIMOTHY COOK

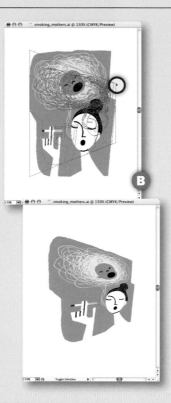

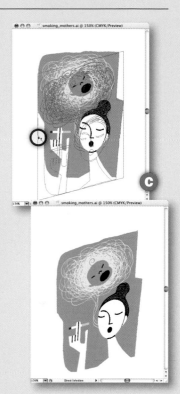

A few shortcuts using the Free Transform tool enable you to manipulate objects with effects similar to those found in the Distort & Transform menu (Effect > Distort & Transform). The advantage of using these shortcuts is that you can work directly on the artboard without resorting to manipulating the object through a dialog box.

A *Free Distort:* With the object(s) selected, choose the Free Transform tool and click on a corner handle of the bounding box *first.* Then hold down the Cmd (Ctrl) key while dragging to distort the object. Using this shortcut is much better than using the Free Distort effect, which forces you to manipulate the object without any context of how the object interacts with other objects on the artboard.

B *Perspective:* With the object(s) selected, choose the Free Transform tool and click on a corner handle of the bounding box *first.* Then hold down Cmd-Option (Ctrl-Alt)-Shift while dragging to create a quick perspective effect. While not as convincing as using the 3D effects found on the Effect menu, in certain instances where the perspective doesn't need to be too convincing and speed is a priority, this shortcut can come in very handy.

C *Shear:* Although Shear has its own tool in the toolbox and is not an effect, using the Transform tool to create a shear has the advantage of being easily accessible with a shortcut key (E) as well as being able to manipulate an object with other effects as well.

With the object(s) selected, choose the Free Transform tool and click on a middle handle of the bounding box *first.* Then hold down the Cmd (Ctrl) key while dragging to shear the object. ⌨

Making Curves, Loops, and Curls

When it comes to creating curves, loops, and curls, you need to keep two principles in mind: 1) a perfect circle created with the Illustrator Ellipse tool is accomplished with just *four* anchor points, and 2) less is more.

Learning Curves

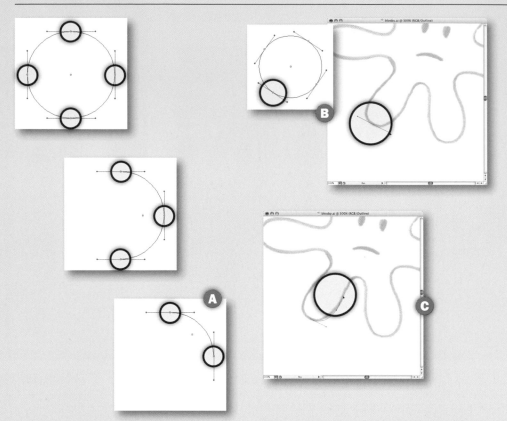

If you've ever tried to draw a perfect circle with the Pen tool, you soon realize what an impossible task it is. Using too many anchor points actually makes it harder to create a smooth curve because of the numerous adjustments that need to be made to each Bézier direction point. However, a circle created with the Ellipse tool is both visually and mathematically perfect, and yet is created with only four anchor points. By removing segments from the circle, you also discover that it takes only three anchor points to create a half circle and only two anchor points to create a 90° curve **A**. So instead of reinventing the wheel (or circle in this case), why not use the same principles when creating curves, loops, and curls?

1. Tracing this object from a scanned template with the Pen tool, we started by creating a short curve. If it takes only two anchor points to create a 90° curve, you can then assume that you should be able to create the first curve with two anchor points. Also, if you look at how a circle is created, each anchor point is positioned at the apex of the curve, before the curve turns toward another direction **B**.

2. Using the Pen tool, click on the artboard to place the first anchor point and then drag to extend a Bézier directional line. Let go of the mouse button, anticipate where the apex of the curve is, click to create another anchor point, and then drag to extend the Bézier directional point **C**.

3. Move to the next curve, and with the circle in mind, create the third anchor point **D**. As you go around the object creating anchor points, keep in mind the circle and how each segment that you draw is related to it. It's important to remember not to try to make the object look perfect on the first try **E**! At this stage you are creating a solid foundation with the correct placement of the anchor points, and you will modify the curves later. Also, by not worrying about creating a perfect shape initially, you'll end up working faster.

4. After creating the basic shape **F** with the anchor points in approximately the right place, using the Direct Selection tool, click one of the anchor points and pull one of the Bézier direction points to adjust the curve **G**.

5. Even though you created the semicircle with three points, if you can get away with using only two points that's even better! Select the object you just made, copy it (Cmd [Ctrl]-C) and Paste in Back (Cmd [Ctrl]-B). With the pasted object still selected press Cmd (Ctrl)-5 to make the object into a guide. Now select the original object, and with the Pen tool place the cursor over an anchor point you want

to delete. When the small minus sign appears next to the Pen cursor/icon, click to delete the anchor point **H**.

6. By adjusting the Bézier direction points and using the copy of the object as a guide, you can find out if it's possible to create a smoother curve with two points instead of three **I**. If the curve doesn't show any improvement, you always have the copy of the object, which you can revert from a guide to a path, or you can use multiple undos to get back to where you started.

Curve Guides

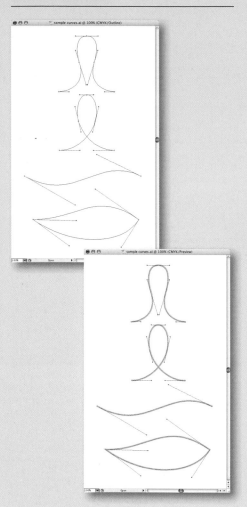

Curling from Circles

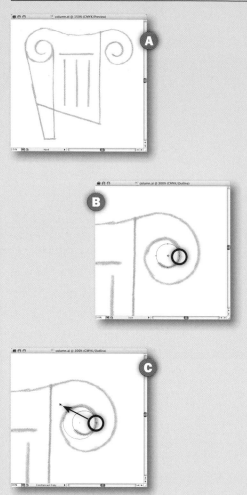

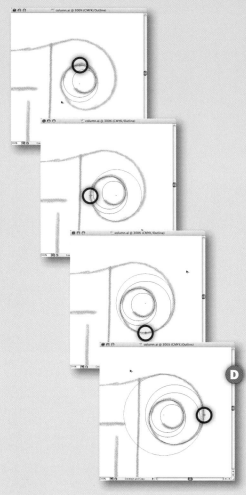

Here are a few guides that show how anchor points are positioned along basic curves and loops.

Although the Spiral tool makes beautiful curls, like other canned effects, many times its results aren't exactly what you are looking for. In these cases, you need to draw the curl yourself.

1. In this example we used a scanned sketch **A** as a template for the curl we'll draw. Using a circle as the starting point, select the circle object, and then select the Scale tool. Click the anchor point that is the apex of the curve (before the curve changes direction) **B**.

2. Hold down the Option (Alt) and Shift keys, and scale a copy of the circle object **C**.

3. Repeat until there are enough circle objects to create all of the curl's segments **D**.

4. Using the Direct Selection tool, delete the unwanted segments. The easiest way to do this is to click the anchor points that are one past the segment you want to keep **E**.

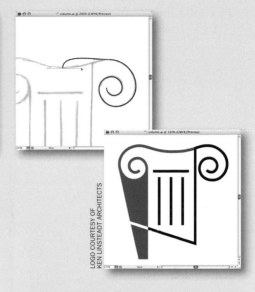

T I P

Curves Based on Circles. Sometimes, you just can't get a curve to look right. Try using a series of circles and create anchor points with the Scissors tool where the circles overlap. Use steps 5 **G** and 6 **H** from the "Curling from Circles" example to join the segments together and then use steps 5 **H** and 6 **I** from the "Learning Curves" example to modify the curve.

5. All you need to do now is join all the path segments together. Eventually, you'll be joining the anchor points together to make a single path, but before you get to that step make sure that the anchor points are actually on top of each other. Although visually you were scaling from an anchor point, you were actually scaling from where your cursor was positioned. If you marquee-select the anchor points and then join them, you might create a path between two points by mistake **F**. Averaging both points together (Cmd-Option

[Ctrl-Alt]-J) is another option; however, the downside is that you slightly throw off the curve you worked so hard to create. A better way is to select each path by the anchor point and use either Snap to Point or Smart Guides (see "Shortcuts to Save You Time" in Chapter 1) to ensure that the anchor points are directly on top of each other **G**.

6. With the Direct Selection tool, marquee-select the overlapping anchor point and press Cmd (Ctrl)-J to join them. If the anchor points are exactly on top of

each other, the Join dialog box should appear **H**. Click Smooth and then OK. Repeat until all segments are joined together.

7. When modifying your new curl using the Bézier direction points, keep in mind that this curl was created with circles and anchor points constrained to a 90° angle. When modifying the curl, you should keep to the same constraint by holding down the Shift key while dragging the Bézier direction point **I**. 🖰

Select Same Strategies

Tired of holding down the Shift key to select the same objects over and over again? Frustrated by the inability to select an object that you can't get to because there are too many objects in the way? Eliminate these hassles and more by using the Select menu commands to streamline your workflow.

The Select Menu

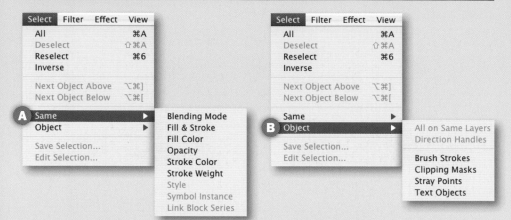

When your artwork becomes more and more complex, it becomes increasingly tedious to use the Selection tools to hunt and click objects or paths with similar attributes. You can use the selection commands in the Select menu as a huge time-saver for this purpose.

A Same: These commands select objects or paths with the same Blending Mode, Fill & Stroke, Fill Color, Opacity, Stroke Color, Stroke Weight, Style, Symbol Instance, or Link Block Series (linked text). Of these, Fill Color, Stroke Color, and Stroke Weight are the most useful for the day-to-day tasks of changing colors while doing different color studies or trying to find the perfect stroke weight for your artwork.

B Object: These commands select objects or paths with Brush Strokes, Clipping Masks, Stray Points, Text Objects, and Link Block Series (linked text). Clipping Masks comes in handy if you start to lose track of the clipping masks you have created, and Stray Points is extremely useful for finding points that don't have a fill or stroke attribute and need to be deleted. Finding stray points is very important if your artwork's dimensions are being defined by the bounding area since unfilled, unstroked points will affect the artwork's size.

Two other selection commands are also available: All on Same Layers (which is more easily done by Option [Alt]-clicking on the layer in the Layers palette) and Direction Handles (we're not quite sure how this is useful).

Select Again

Save Selection

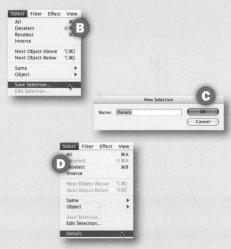

Once you've made a selection, the Reselect command (Cmd [Ctrl]-6) repeats the selection command. For instance, if you need to modify the red in this illustration by David Flaherty, you can direct select the golfer's red shirt **A** and then choose Select > Same > Fill Color, which selects all objects with the same red color **B**. If you also want to change the green color, direct select one of the palm tree leaves **C** and press Cmd (Ctrl)-6 to repeat the selection command (Fill Color) and select all objects with that green color **D**. When doing color studies, this is a fast way to select objects or strokes with similar colors.

Saving a selection can save you a lot of time! Using this example you might want to select all the details in the illustration to hide them so that they won't be distracting while picking colors for the major objects in the illustration. You could put all the details on one layer and then hide the layer. However, what if one of the details is inside a clipping mask or stacked on different layers? Instead, select all the details **A** and choose Select > Save Selection **B**. In the New Selection dialog box, name the selection "Details" **C**. Now all you have to do to select the details is choose Select > Details **D**.

Making Sure Black Is Black

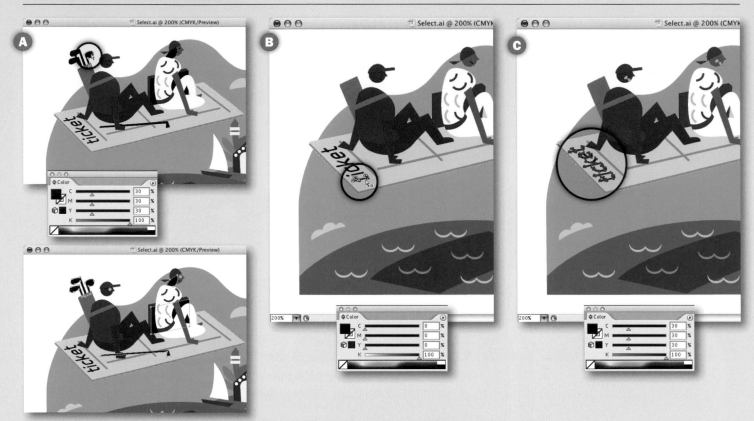

For print work there are many ways to represent black using a mixture of cyan, magenta, yellow, and black (CMYK) ink colors. In Illustrator, the default black is 0 cyan, 0 magenta, 0 yellow, and 100% black. However, when printed, this type of black can appear "flat" or "light," and in instances that don't involve text, a "rich" black is preferred. Rich black is a term that refers to using 100% black with a combination of the three other ink colors to produce a denser or "richer" black.

Depending on your personal preference, there are many, many combinations of rich black. Our preference is 30C, 30M, 30Y, 100K. The important objective is to

ensure that all the objects in your Illustrator file with a black fill use the same color combination, no matter what type of rich black you use. Since black on your monitor looks the same whether you are using a default 100K or a rich black, finding those black objects is the first step. A handy way to do this is to choose Select > Same > Fill Color.

After the artwork is finished and before sending the Illustrator file to your client, you need to find the objects that might have been mistakenly filled with 100K instead of a rich black. To do this, you can follow a simple process of elimination. Select an object filled with a rich black (30C, 30M, 30Y, 100K) **A** and

then choose Select > Same > Fill Color. Once all the objects with the same rich black in your artwork are selected, press Cmd (Ctrl)-3 to hide the objects. Since all the rich black objects are hidden, those black objects left in your artwork can be changed to a rich black. Select another black object **B** and press Cmd (Ctrl)-6 to select Same Fill Colors again **C**. In the Color palette change the object's fill to rich black and hide those objects. Repeat these steps as many times as necessary until there are no black objects left on the artboard, then use Object > Show All (Cmd-Option [Ctrl-Alt]-3) to unhide all of the rich black objects.

Finding Nothing

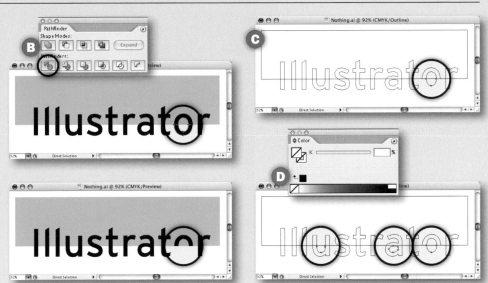

There are times when using the Select command can help you find objects with no fill or stroke attribute so you can delete them. For this example, create a rectangle and lay text (type *Illustrator*) on top of it **A**. Then outline the text and apply the

Divide Pathfinder filter to it **B**. Next, select a segment of the "O" and press Cmd (Ctrl)-3 to hide it. After the segment is hidden you'll see that the Divide filter created unwanted objects with no fill or stroke that you want to get rid of (since the object might be selected by mistake later) **C**. If the Divide filter created one problematical

object with no fill or stroke, odds are that the filter created more of them. Select the offending object and choose Select > Same > Fill Color. Even though the object had no fill attribute, the Select command selects all objects with no fill **D**. After the no-fill objects are selected, delete them all. 🔲

Anatomy of an Infographic

This beautifully rendered and very complex information graphic was created through the use of symbols, graphic styles, and the Appearance palette. In this section we dissect the different elements to show how Illustrator is indispensable for this type of artwork.

Symbols

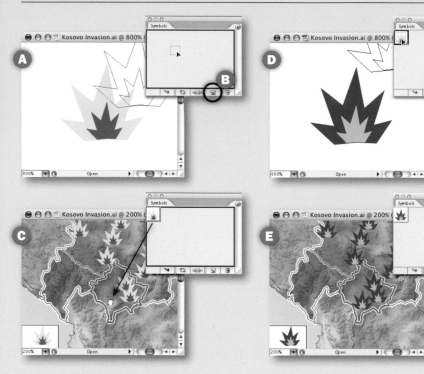

Symbols were used to indicate the reported strikes and the type of Yugoslav bases, as well as indicators for the NATO bases, primary bases, and location icons. Using the Symbols palette is natural for this type of work because of its capability to modify a single piece of artwork and update numerous symbol instances of that art automatically.

1. Here, an explosion icon was created and dragged to the Symbols palette to create a new symbol of it **A**. You can also create a new symbol by selecting the artwork and clicking the New Symbol button at the bottom of the Symbols palette **B**.

2. A thumbnail of the icon appears in the palette, which you can then drag to the artboard for placement **C**.

3. After making modifications to the original icon artwork, you can select the artwork, and, by holding down the Option (Alt) key, you can drag the artwork on top of the explosion icon thumbnail in the Symbols palette **D**. This updates the explosion icon symbol in the Symbols palette and at the same time updates every instance of the icon symbol in the file **E**. For more on symbols, see "Create a Logo Sheet with Symbols" in the Supplement.

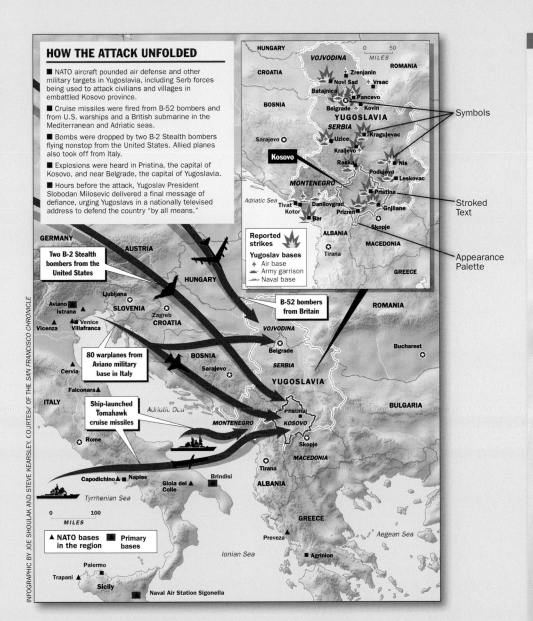

HOW THE ATTACK UNFOLDED

■ NATO aircraft pounded air defense and other military targets in Yugoslavia, including Serb forces being used to attack civilians and villages in embattled Kosovo province.

■ Cruise missiles were fired from B-52 bombers and from U.S. warships and a British submarine in the Mediterranean and Adriatic seas.

■ Bombs were dropped by two B-2 Stealth bombers flying nonstop from the United States. Allied planes also took off from Italy.

■ Explosions were heard in Pristina, the capital of Kosovo, and near Belgrade, the capital of Yugoslavia.

■ Hours before the attack, Yugoslav President Slobodan Milosevic delivered a final message of defiance, urging Yugoslavs in a nationally televised address to defend the country "by all means."

Two B-2 Stealth bombers from the United States

80 warplanes from Aviano military base in Italy

Ship-launched Tomahawk cruise missiles

B-52 bombers from Britain

Reported strikes
Yugoslav bases
✈ Air base
⚓ Army garrison
⚓ Naval base

▲ NATO bases in the region   ■ Primary bases

Symbols

Stroked Text

Appearance Palette

INFOGRAPHIC BY JOE SHOULAK AND STEVE KEARSLEY. COURTESY OF THE SAN FRANCISCO CHRONICLE

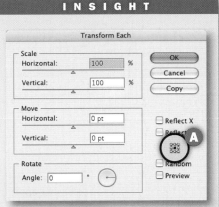

Transform Each. Anyone who has ever worked on a map knows that after painstakingly positioning multiple location dots, you inevitably wish you had made them just a little bit bigger or smaller. Selecting them all and resizing them will move the dots out of position because a single transformation can only have one origin point. If the dots were made with a symbol, you could resize and replace the symbol, but that's a bit of a hassle. This situation is perfect for using the Transform Each dialog box.

1. Select the dots. We suggest that you select the dots and then save them as a selection using Select > Save Selection. For more on selection features, see "Select Same Strate-gies" earlier in this chapter.

2. Press Cmd-Option (Ctrl-Alt)-Shift-D to bring up the Transform Each dialog box or choose Object > Transform > Transform Each.

3. In the Transform Each dialog box you can choose to scale, move, and rotate objects. For the location dots, try scaling from the center of each dot by clicking the center reference point in the reference pane **A**.

Remember, the objects you would like to transform need to be ungrouped.

Stroke Your Text for Better Legibility

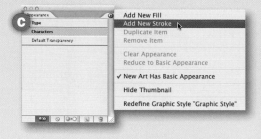

Information graphics are not effective if they can't be read and comprehended quickly. Unfortunately, infographics often entail placing text over a raster image, such as a topographic map or photograph, or over complex vector graphics, such as cutaways and architectural renderings. Because the text is often very small, legibility is hampered by these nonsolid backgrounds. Artists often put a thin stroke around the text to enable it to be more easily read by standing out from the background. The problem with using the Stroke palette to add a stroke around the text is that the stroke is stacked on top of the text, squeezing the font's appearance and affecting the text's legibility **A**. A more efficient method is to add a stroke behind the text by using the Appearance palette.

Here are the steps to follow:

1. Create your first text label in your desired font and point size. Just use the default black fill with no stroke for placement, although the fill will change later **B**.

2. With the Selection tool, select your text and fill it with None (to find out why see "Insight: Text and the Appearance Palette"). In the Appearance palette, select Add New Stroke from the palette menu **C**.

3. The Appearance palette enables you to reshuffle items, much like the Layers palette. Move the new stroke attribute below the fill attribute **D**.

4. By default a 1 pt stroke attribute will be added to the Appearance palette as well as a no-fill attribute. Make sure the new stroke attribute is selected in the Appearance palette. Adjust the stroke weight in

the Stroke palette. The value will depend on the size of your text and how you want the text to look. We used 1.25 pt for our stroke (and since the stroke is stacked in back of the letterform, it actually appears as a .625 pt stroke) **E**.

5. With the new stroke still selected in the Appearance palette, choose a stroke color from the Swatches or Color palette. For a more subtle effect, add a 40% opacity to the stroke attribute in the Transparency palette.

6. Next, even though the text is black (the way we want it), since we are planning to make a Graphic Style from the text's appearance, we need to specify a black fill in the Appearance palette. Select the Fill attribute in the Appearance palette. Choose your desired color—in this case, black **F**.

Text and the Appearance Palette.
Text does not work in quite the same way as other objects in the Appearance palette. It is important to remember when working with text in the Appearance palette that text acts like its own group, with its own fill and stroke attribute. However, the fill and stroke attributes don't show up as layers like other objects. To make things more confusing, once a new stroke or fill has been added to a text object in the Appearance palette, the only way to change the text's own fill and stroke is by selecting the text with the Text tool, not through the Appearance palette as you could before you added the new stroke! *But wait.* Before you give up on using this invaluable feature, let's take it one step at a time.

1. **A** Text created with the Text tool has a black fill and no stroke. In the Appearance palette, there is a Type layer, but no fill or stroke information.

2. **B** A new 10 pt stroke is created in the Appearance palette and given an orange color attribute. The stroke attribute is moved beneath the fill None attribute layer.

3. **C** The fill attribute is changed to yellow. The appearance of the stroke is beneath the yellow fill.

4. **D** However, if you move the stroke attribute under the Characters in the stacking order, something peculiar hap-

pens. Zooming in, you can see a little bit of black peeking around the edges of the yellow fill of the text.

5. **E** Highlighting the text with the Text tool reveals that the text still has a black fill attribute, which is what is causing the faint halo.

6. **F** Using the Text tool to give the text fill an attribute of None gets rid of the black halo since the text is no longer black.

Conclusion: When using the Appearance palette to enhance text, it's best to give the text a fill and stroke of None, and use the Appearance palette to control the attributes so you can manipulate them easily.

Troubleshooting with the Appearance Palette

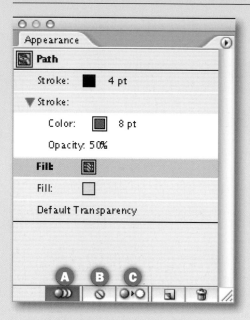

The Appearance palette gives you the ultimate overview window into every attribute that has to do with a path, objects, or groups of objects in your file. As we mentioned earlier in "Stroke Your Text for Better Legibility," the Appearance palette comes in very handy for adding multiple stacked strokes to any path, object, or text. But it also acts as troubleshooter when you can't figure out why an object isn't behaving the way it should (maybe unbeknownst to you it's part of a group, a compound path, or a clipping mask). Located at the bottom of the Appearance palette (and also in the palette menu) are three buttons that can not only help you with a stubborn object, but can also help in the creation of new objects.

A *New Art Has Basic Appearance:* This toggle button is on by default. When this button is on, any artwork that you create will have a basic appearance (a single stroke stacked on top of a single fill) even

if the last object or path that was created or selected has a complex appearance. In this example, a complex object was created using multiple strokes and fill attributes. With the button turned *off*, every object created afterward also has the same stroke and fill attributes. With the button turned *on*, however, any object created afterward has a basic one-stroke, one-fill attribute regardless of the objects selected or created beforehand.

B *Clear Appearance:* This is the ultimate reset button. When you select text, paths, or objects and then click this button, the appearance will reduce to a single stroke and fill, both with an attribute of None. It's very handy for the most stubborn of objects or paths.

C *Reduce to Basic Appearance:* This button reduces the appearance of any complex object to the topmost fill and topmost stroke in the stacking order.

Multiple Fills. Not only can you add multiple strokes to text and objects, but you can add multiple fills as well. While the practical uses of multiple fills don't rival those of multiple strokes, they can come in handy for a project now and then. The interesting thing about multiple fills is that you can apply an effect to one fill but not another to create elements such as those shown in the figures. To do so, simply select the object with the Selection tool, and then select the fill you want to manipulate in the Appearance palette. Choose your desired effect from the Effect menu. If you want to change the color or stroke weight of a fill (or stroke), select your object, select the fill/stroke, and change the color or weight in the appropriate palette. To tweak the settings of an effect, make your selections and double-click the effect **A** to bring up the appropriate dialog box.

Targeting and the Appearance Palette

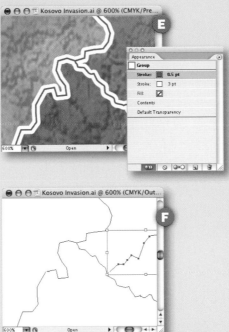

T I P

Targeting Layers. Not only can groups be targeted and attributes added through the Appearance palette, but layers can too. In the Layers palette, click the small button on the right in the layer you want to target **H**. Looking at the Appearance palette, you'll see that the layer is now targeted, and any attributes added will affect the objects on that layer as a whole **I**.

To make borderlines for the map, you need to create a double, stacked stroke. Using the Appearance palette to stack individual strokes **A** won't produce the desired effect of the strokes appearing on top of the border strokes underneath **B**. The solution is to create stacked strokes by "targeting" a group via the Appearance palette.

1. Create the border paths and use a fill and stroke attribute of None. Then group the paths **C**.

2. Select the group and then use the Appearance palette to add two new strokes from the palette menu **D**.

3. Give the stroke on top a width attribute of **.5** pt and a color attribute of **50**% black. Give the stroke on the bottom a width attribute of **3** pt and a color attribute of white **E**.

4. By targeting a group, the new strokes are added to the whole group instead of to individual paths. As a bonus, you can create and paste paths into the group by using the Direct Selection tool, clicking on one of the paths in the group, and then pasting in front/back **F**. Once part of the group, the pasted path takes on all of the group's attributes **G**.

Using Graphic Styles

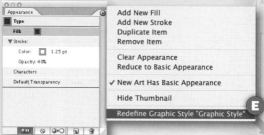

Not to be confused with Text or Paragraph Styles (which will be covered later in Chapter 5, "Designing with Illustrator"), Graphic Styles allow you to apply a whole set of appearance attributes (fill, stroke, transparency, etc.) to objects or groups of objects.

For this map, Graphic Styles were used for the outlined text and borderlines. Open the Graphic Styles palette, and with the Selection tool, select the text or border that was modified with the Appearance palette **A**. Click the New Graphic Style button at the bottom of the Graphic Styles palette **B** (or choose New Graphic Style from the palette menu).

To apply the text style, create other text labels and select the text with a Selection tool. Then click the style thumbnail in the Graphic Styles palette **C**.

To modify a style, Option (Alt)-drag an object with the modified attributes on top of the thumbnail in the Graphic Styles palette **D**. To modify a currently selected graphic style, change the attributes in the Appearance palette and choose Redefine Graphic Style from the palette menu **E**. 🂠

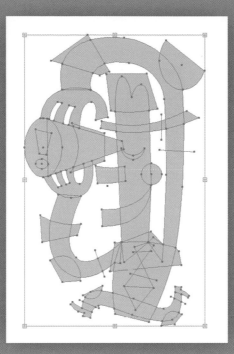

Non-Destructive Color Panes with Live Paint

Create butt-joined color panes without resorting to masks or Pathfinder effects.

1. Introducing Live Paint

With Illustrator CS2 a brand-new feature named Live Paint was introduced. Although similar in name to another feature introduced at the same time called Live Trace, they have very little in common. Live Trace is like Stream-line (a widely used older Adobe appli-cation that converted bitmapped images to vector objects) on steroids, whereas Live Paint offers a different way to work with vector objects and paths.

We intentionally say "a different way" instead of "a new way" because "new" implies that you will have to change or learn a new workflow to use this feature—and really, who has time to do that? Will falling in love with the Live Paint feature make you radically change the way you work in order to use it? Possibly, but first things first. We'll show you how you can use Live Paint in your *existing* workflow.

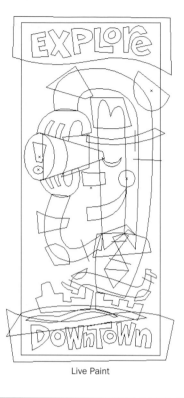

Live Paint

Pathfinder

Let's deconstruct this fun piece of banner artwork by Von Glitschka to show how, without much effort, Live Paint can work for you. Here are two versions of the same piece of artwork **A** (note that the gradient in the background is removed to show a clearer view of the work). Although visually identical, if you view the artwork in Outline mode **B**, you'll see that they were built in totally different ways. The example on the left was created using Live Paint, whereas the one on the right was done traditionally—using Pathfinder effects.

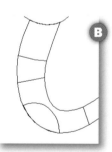

2. Examine How the Arm Is Built

Focusing on the arm shows that the Live Paint version **A** is actually made up of the same paths used *before* the Pathfinder Divide effect was applied to create the more traditional version **B**. The advantage of using Live Paint is clearly shown here **C**, where you can move and manipulate the "elbow patch" within the arm in the Live Paint version, whereas the Pathfinder version **D** shows that dividing the paths leaves you no flexibility whatsoever.

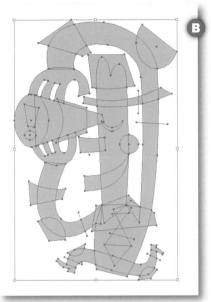

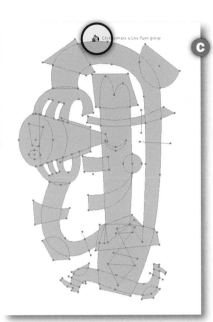

3. Make a Group with Live Paint

To use Live Paint you first need to make a Live Paint "group." A Live Paint group is simply any number of objects that you have selected to utilize this mode. Live Paint will only work on this grouping of objects (although you can have multiple groups); however, it is very easy to add or subtract from this group.

Two tools are associated with Live Paint: the Live Paint Bucket (K) **A** and the Live Paint Selection tool (Shift-L). To create a Live Paint group, select an object or a number of objects **B**, move the Live Paint Bucket tool over a selected object **C**, and click. The objects that you selected are now a Live Paint group. Another way to create a Live Paint group is to select the objects and choose Object > Live Paint > Make **D**.

Clicking on a Live Paint group with the normal Selection tool shows that this type of group has a different style bounding box than normal objects (notice the fancy squares) **E**.

In this example, we hid the background and headline artwork, selected the main figure, and then used the Live Paint Bucket to create a Live Paint group.

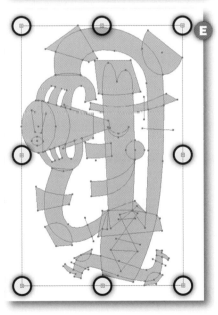

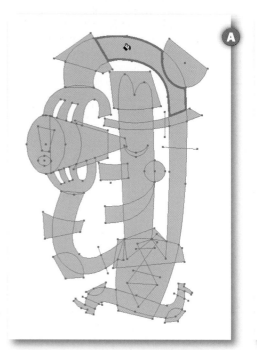

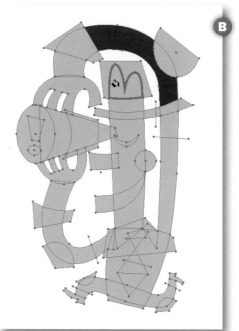

4. Use Live Paint Groups and the Paint Bucket

Now select the Live Paint Bucket tool and pass over the group **A**. Notice that there is an "over" state for each area that is "divided" by a path, indicated by a heavy red stroke (see "Tip: Adding to a Live Paint Group"). Choose a fill color and click on an area. The Live Paint Bucket fills the area with that color **B**. Not only can you fill an area with a color, but you can also fill an area with a gradient or pattern. When you hold down the Shift key, the Live Paint Bucket's icon changes to a brush, which enables you to fill "edges" with the stroke color or pattern. By holding down the Option (Alt) key, you can temporarily change the Bucket to the Eyedropper tool.

T I P

Adding to a Live Paint Group. You can add an object to a Live Paint group in a few ways, but the easiest is to create a new object, cut it to the clipboard, and then use the Direct Selection tool to select one of the objects already in the group. Paste in Front or Back (Cmd [Ctrl]-F or Cmd [Ctrl]-B), and the object on the clipboard becomes part of the group.

T I P

Painting Multiple Objects. Using the Live Paint Bucket, click on an area to fill it with a color, and while still holding down the button, drag to adjacent areas to fill those with color too!

T I P

The Paint Bucket's Not So Subtle Edge. The default highlight edge for the Live Paint Bucket tool is a whopping 4 points! As you can imagine, that makes rolling over small areas somewhat problematic. To change the weight, double-click the Paint Bucket tool, which brings up the Live Paint Bucket Options dialog box. In this dialog box you can change the stroke width and change the color if you are so inclined.

Live Paint Bucket Options

Options
☑ Paint Fills ☐ Paint Strokes

☑ Highlight
Color: ▮▮▮ Red
Width: 4 pt

OK
Cancel
Tips

5. Use the Live Paint Selection Tool

The Live Paint Selection tool might be a more familiar type of tool for long-time Illustrator users, and in some ways it is much more efficient. Like the normal Selection tools, click an area you want to fill (or multiple areas using the Shift key), and then click a color swatch to fill it. However, unlike normal Selection tools, you cannot drag a swatch to the selection to fill it. This workflow works well but takes a little time getting used to mainly because of a hideous looking screen that shows the highlighted area but also obscures whatever changes you've made until you've deselected the area. The Live Paint Selection tool can also highlight edges, although using the Live Paint feature for strokes gives you inconsistent results (see "Caution: Live Paint Strokes" in step 6)

One interesting feature of the Live Paint Selection tool is that it allows you to select an area and then delete it using the Delete (Backspace) key. This feature's usefulness is a little questionable since not only do you have to remember to delete the fill *and* the stroke, but by taking out whole sections, it makes editing a path a little less flexible (see "Tip: Use None Instead of Delete").

T I P

Use None Instead of Delete. Although it might be tempting to do lote areas that are not in use, it's better just to give them a fill of None. That way the offending areas are basically invisible, and you still have a whole path, which makes it easier to manipulate if you need to later.

6. Manipulate Paths: Release and Expand Live Paint Groups

The beauty of the Live Paint mode is that objects in a Live Paint group can be manipulated **A** like any other object on the artboard, either individually with the Direct Selection tool or all at once with the Selection tool.

After creating your artwork using Live Paint you can choose to expand the Live Paint group into ordinary vector paths by selecting Object > Live Paint > Expand. Illustrator splits up the fills and stokes of the objects into their new appearance. Of course after you do this, you'll lose a lot of flexibility to edit your paths, and production-wise it's not necessary.

If you change your mind and want to revert the Live Paint group to its original paths, just select Object > Live Paint > Release. However, the problem with releasing a Live Paint group is that the original objects lose fill and stroke appearances. ▦

CAUTION

Live Paint Strokes. Unfortunately, the end caps of a Live Paint stroke will only conform to an area if the area is at a 90 degree angle.

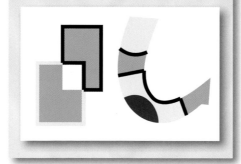

Convert Engravings into Line Art with Live Trace

Use one piece of art to create another.

1. Create a New Illustrator Document

Choose File > New. In the New Document dialog box, enter the Name, Width and Height, Orientation, and Color Mode.

2. Place Your Raster Artwork

Choose File > Place and select your desired raster file. It doesn't matter whether or not you link your file. Note that you can also open the artwork and execute a live trace.

The raster image of our dodo happens to be a 300 dpi JPEG file. You can also use other common raster formats such as TIFF, PSD, or PDF. Note that in many cases you'll get different results depending on the resolution of your raster image. We'll show you the results of using 72 dpi, 150 dpi, 300 dpi, and 600 dpi images (see step 3). The more detailed the raster image, the more noticeable the differences.

72dpi

150dpi

300dpi

600dpi

3. Select Your Raster Image

Select your raster image and do one of the following:

- *Trace with a preset:* In the Control palette, click the Tracing presets and options button and select a preset that most closely matches your raster image. Once you select the preset, the tracing process starts.

- *Trace with the default setting:* Click the Live Trace button in the Control palette. You can also choose Object > Live Trace > Make.

- *Specify your tracing options first, then trace:* In the Control palette, click the Tracing presets and options button and select Tracing Options. You can also choose Object > Live Trace > Tracing Options. (For details on the various options, see "Tip: Tracing Options.") Specify your desired tracing options, and then click the Trace button in the dialog box.

Note that if you modify any settings, the preset changes to Custom. To save your custom preset, click Save Preset, name it, and click OK.

We chose to use the default setting, which uses a Black and White mode. The figure shows the same setting applied to four different resolutions.

T I P

Tracing Options. The options are extensive, but luckily a good number are pretty self-explanatory. Here's a brief explanation of some of the more obscure options:

Mode: Choose Color, Grayscale, or Black and White for the tracing.

Threshold: Enter a value for Black and White mode. Any pixels lighter than the value convert to white; darker pixels convert to black.

Palette: Specifies a color palette for Color and Grayscale mode. Illustrator automatically determines color. You can also choose any open swatch library.

Blur: Blurs the raster image prior to tracing to eliminate jagged edges. Can result in smoother edges, but can also result in a less than accurate tracing.

Resample: Changes the resolution in the raster image before tracing. We don't recommend changing this setting. Make sure your raster image is at your desired resolution before placing it in Illustrator.

Path Fitting: Controls how close the tracing follows the raster image. Use a lower number to make the path fit snugly.

Raster and *Vector:* Choose how you want your raster image and tracing to display onscreen. Note that this setting does not affect the actual artwork—just how you view it onscreen.

Grayscale

Hand Drawn Sketch

Inked Drawing

Detailed Illustration

4. Adjust Your Tracing Results

Not thrilled with the results? Select the tracing and select a different preset in the Control palette. You can also adjust other basic settings there as well. If you need more industrial-strength changes, click the Tracing Options Dialog button in the Control palette to access all of the settings.

To delete the tracing but retain your raster image, select your tracing and choose Object > Live Trace > Release.

5. Convert Your Tracing to Paths

If you truly want the benefits of a vector image, you'll probably want to convert your tracing to paths or to a Live Paint object (for more on Live Paint see the section "Non-Destructive Color Panes with Live Paint"). Make sure your tracing is the way you want it, because you can't make any tracing adjustments once you've made the conversion. To convert the dodo tracing to paths, select it and click the Expand button in the Control palette. You can also choose Object > Live Trace > Expand. The tracing converts to a conglomeration of grouped paths.

Note that you can also trace and expand in one fell swoop by choosing Object > Live Trace > Make and Expand.

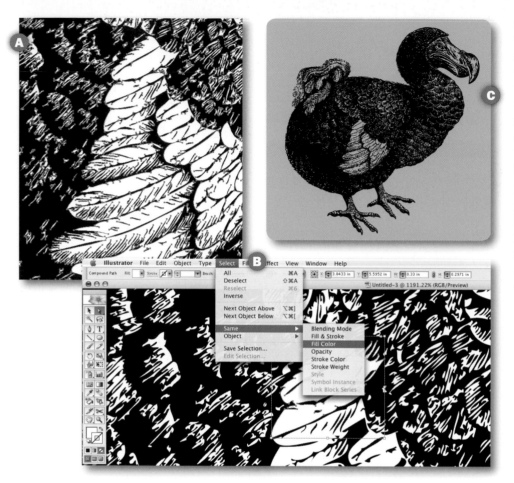

6. Eliminate White Areas

To make the white areas transparent so the background color will show through, zoom in **A** and select one of the white areas, and then choose Select > Same > Fill Color **B**. All of the white areas are selected. Press Delete (Backspace) and presto, "holes" now exist where once there were opaque white fills **C**.

If you are not happy with the results, you can always place the raster image file and use the drawing tools (Pen, Pencil, and so on) to manually trace over the image. See the earlier section on "Becoming a Pen Master" if your digital drawing skills are rusty. 🁢

INSIGHT

Live Tracing a Sketch. Artist Timothy Cook, previously an aficionado of Adobe Streamline (unfortunately no longer supported), recently decided to put Live Trace to the test. He scanned a hand-drawn sketch at 300 dpi and saved it as a TIFF in Bitmap mode. He then imported it into Illustrator (see figure on left) and executed the Live Trace command using the Detailed Illustration preset with the default settings intact (see figure on right). The preset applied a slight Gaussian blur to smooth out the overly pixilated edges and then traced the artwork. Timothy was pleased with both the quality of the results and the short amount of time it took to execute the trace. Sure beats manually tracing it with the Pen tool.

TIMOTHY COOK

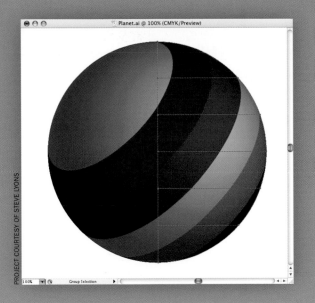

PROJECT COURTESY OF STEVE LYONS

Create 3D Planets

Use Pathfinder and the 3D Revolve effect to create your own universe.

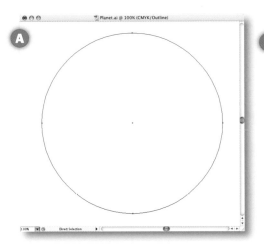

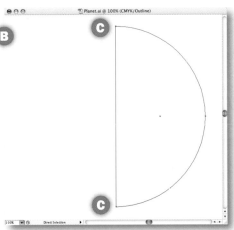

1. Create a Half Circle

Using the Ellipse tool, create a circle that will be the starting point of your planet **A**. Since the 3D Revolve effect rotates artwork from the left axis **B**, delete the left half of the circle, and then join the open anchor points **C**.

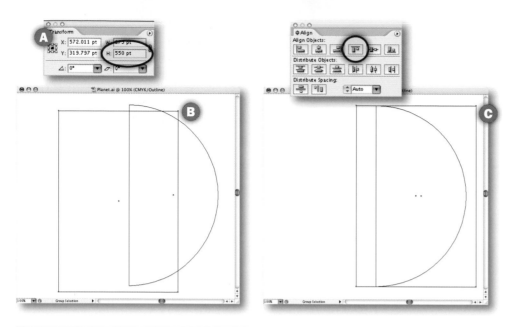

2. Create a Rectangle

Select the half circle and look in the Control or Transform palettes for the height measurement of the half circle **A**. Using the Rectangle tool, create a rectangle that is the same height as the half circle **B**. Now select both the half circle and the rectangle, and click the Vertical Align Top icon in the Align palette to make sure that the two objects' tops are aligned. Then overlap the rectangle on the left and right sides **C**.

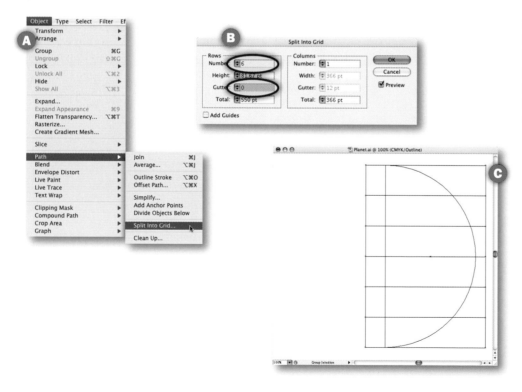

3. Divide the Rectangle

Select the rectangle and then choose Object > Path > Split Into Grid **A**. In the Split Into Grid dialog box, enter **6** for Number of Rows and set the Gutter to **0 B**. The result is six neatly divided rows **C**.

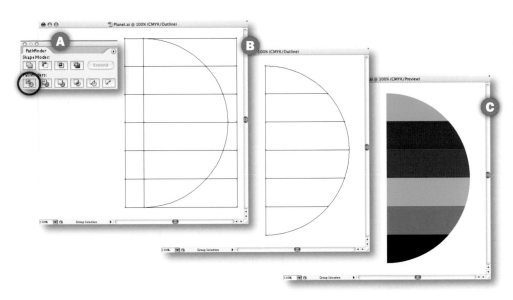

4. Divide and Color the Half Circle

Select all the objects, and in the Path-finder palette, click the Divide path-finder **A**. Next, using the Direct Selection tool, delete the extraneous paths **B**. Direct select the individual half circle paths and fill them with different colors **C**.

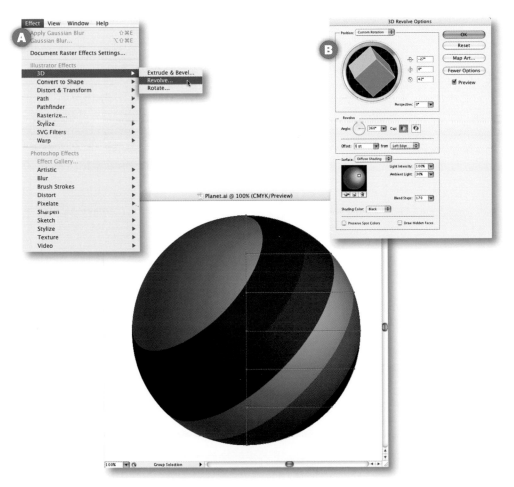

5. Use 3D Revolve to Create the Planet

For the final step, use the Selection tool, select the half circle, and then choose Effect > 3D > Revolve **A**. In the 3D Revolve Options dialog box, select the Preview check box and drag the cube in the Position panel **B** to rotate your newly formed planet. 🖐

INSIGHT

Revolving Grouped Objects. One convenient feature of using the Divide Pathfinder to create the bands of color is that the divided shapes are automatically grouped. When objects are grouped, selected, and one of the 3D effects is applied, the effect treats the object as one unit and rotates, revolves, and extrudes them as one. If the objects are not grouped, the 3D effect treats them all separately, with unpredictable results as shown here.

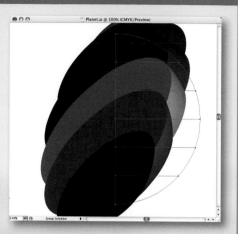

TIP

Create a Flying Saucer. Using the same concept as creating the planet, you can also create other objects. A flying saucer was created using this cross section of grouped objects and the 3D Revolve effect.

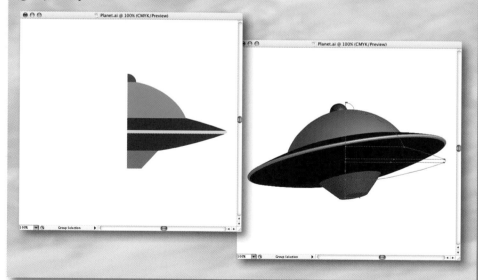

TIP

Adding to a 3D Object. Remember to group your object(s) before you apply a 3D effect (even if it's only a single object), thereby making it easy to add to the object after the 3D effect has been applied.

1. Select the object(s) you want to the 3D object and cut them to add to the clipboard.

2. Using the Direct Selection tool, select the object that has the 3D effect applied to it.

3. Paste in Front (Cmd [Ctrl]-F) to make the objects on the clipboard part of the group and in turn part of the 3D object.

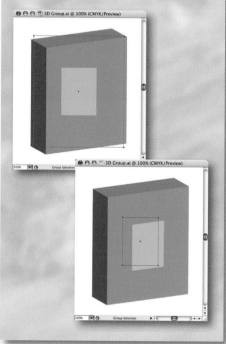

3

MASKS AND BLEND EFFECTS

Using and Understanding Masks, Gradients, and Blend Effects

I N THE PAST if someone gave you a pile of digitally produced artwork it was a snap to divide the images easily into two piles—those created in Photoshop and those done in Illustrator. Soft, shaded, semi-opaque objects were evidence of a Photoshop experience, whereas crisp, clean vector lines were obviously the handiwork of Illustrator. Not so today. While Photoshop has garnered the ability to create vector shapes, so has Illustrator been given incredible tools and methods to give line art three dimensionality through techniques such as masks, blends, gradients, and true transparency.

Masks and Transparency

Masks are one of the most powerful and misunderstood features in Illustrator. Masks are extremely versatile in what they can do, and yet for many, masks are a hard concept to wrap their head around. A mask, no matter what program it is created in, basically

selectively shows and hides certain elements. Depending on the type of mask you use, this could mean hiding some elements completely or just partially. For example, in the project, "Masks Within Masks," we show you how to fit a pattern within a shirt and then a shirt within a body using clipping masks. The powerful opacity mask enables you to create a transparent effect whereby your background partially shows through your elements. In this chapter, masks of all sorts—clipping, layer clipping, and opacity—will be presented in detail.

Gradients and Blends

If you desire more of a three-dimensional look to your Illustrator art, using gradients and blends, often paired with masks, is the way to go. We'll show you how to overcome one of the biggest difficulties—creating multiple gradients that intersect seamlessly into one another. We'll also describe the instances where

blends are actually preferred over gradients. In the section, "Blending and Masks," we'll use a combination of blends and masks to give a statue her voluptuous undulations.

We hope that, after you've perused this chapter, you'll be inclined to use masks, gradients, and blends with less hesitation and even a tad of enthusiasm.

Masks Explained

As we mentioned in the introduction, many people are baffled by Illustrator's masking capabilities. There have been numerous attempts over the years to make using masks easier, the latest being the introduction of the "layer clipping mask." In this section we'll introduce the two basic types of masks and describe the pros and cons of each.

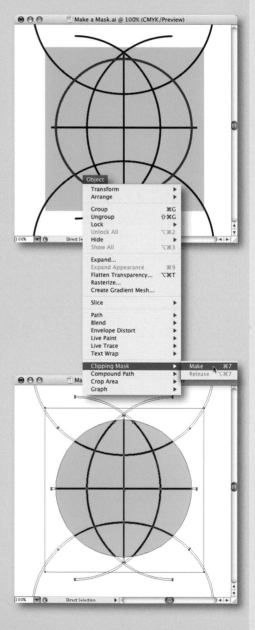

Clipping Mask or Mask

Masks have been around since the earliest versions of Illustrator, but in version 9, "masks" became "clipping masks." The functionality is exactly the same; only the name was changed. However, being the artistic nonconformists that we are, when we refer to masks in this book, we are referring to clipping masks.

You can create clipping masks from any type of vector object: paths, compound shapes, or text objects. In short, a mask is a group of objects with the topmost object "masking" all objects below it in the group.

An easy analogy would be to compare a mask to a box of playing cards. The box represents the group, and the cards within the box are the objects. The top card is always the ace (or mask), and the cards beneath it (the objects) can be shuffled in any order.

To create a clipping mask, begin by positioning the object you'd like to function as the mask on top (in the stacking order) of the object(s) you want to mask out. Remember, the easiest way to change an object's stacking order is by using the Paste in Front/Back command (see "Tip: Arranging Objects Inside Masks"). Then select all objects and press Cmd (Ctrl)-7, or use the contextual menu and choose Make Clipping Mask, or choose Object > Clipping Mask > Make.

Making a clipping mask groups the objects together and, more important, clears the fill and stroke attributes from the top object being used as the mask. Even though releasing the clipping mask (Cmd-Option [Ctrl-Alt]-7) will ungroup the objects, the mask object's original fill/stroke attributes will not return.

Layer Clipping Masks

A layer clipping mask is almost identical to a regular clipping mask with a couple of notable exceptions. With a layer clipping mask the masking object resides as the top-most object in the layer. As you add artwork to that layer, the objects become masked as long as you position the artwork's layer underneath the layer clipping mask in the stacking order. The biggest difference, however, is that a layer clipping mask is not automatically grouped.

Since a layer clipping mask depends on using one mask per layer, its usefulness greatly depends on your workflow and the type of work that you do. For involved work that requires a number of masks, using layer clipping masks might prove cumbersome due to the number of layers you'll need to produce. Also, since the layer clipping masks are not grouped, it might be harder to identify masked objects with a click of the Selection tool as you can with a regular clipping mask.

To create a layer clipping mask go to the Layers palette and click the triangle on the layer to reveal its contents. Make sure that the object you want to be the mask is on top of the stacking order for that layer. Click the layer name (not the object) and either choose Make Clipping Mask from the palette menu or click the Make/Release Clipping Mask button at the bottom of the Layers palette **A.** 🏛

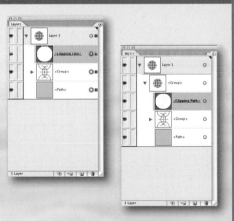

Opacity Masks

An opacity mask is a curious hybrid of the layer mask function in Photoshop and the clipping mask function in Illustrator. Although the implementation of this feature is a bit confusing, once you understand it, opacity masks could become one of your favorite features in Illustrator.

What's an Opacity Mask?

Unlike regular masks, which are defined by the physical area and shape of a vector path, opacity masks (like Photoshop's layer mask) are defined by the positive (white) and negative (black) space, or any shade or gradient in between. This means your mask can be defined by a soft edge, gradient, or black and white piece of artwork—even photographs. If you've ever tried to unsuccessfully overlay two gradients on top of each other, or fade a gradient into two or more different colors, then opacity masks are made for you.

Where Is the Opacity Mask?

Instead of a whole new palette just for opacity masks, the feature is located in the Transparency palette—most likely because there is some "transparency" involved. Whatever. To access opacity mask options, click the arrow in the right corner **A** of the Transparency palette to open the palette menu and choose Show Options **B**.

Create an Opacity Mask

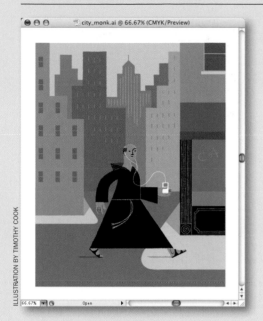

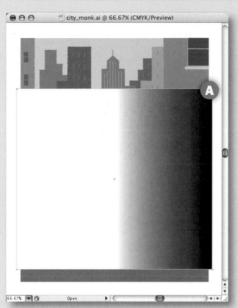

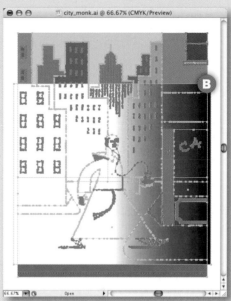

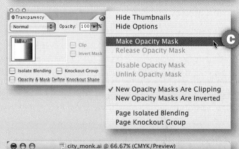

To create an opacity mask, make an object and place it on top of the object(s) you would like to mask. Fill the top object with a gradient **A**. Although opacity masks can be filled with any color, it's best to use black and white. When made into an opacity mask, colors will be translated to their grayscale equivalent anyway, so instead of guessing how a color will translate, you might as well start off in black and white. Now select both objects **B** and on the Transparency palette menu choose Make Opacity Mask **C** (no, there isn't a shortcut key or menu item—this feature is very well hidden). The result is an object that fades to nothing **D**. If you place a gradient filled object below the opacity masked object, the object with the opacity mask will blend right into it **E**!

Using Opacity Masks

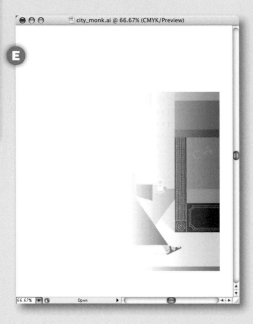

Working with opacity masks after they are created can be a little tricky. Familiarity with how layer masks work in Photoshop is helpful since there are many similarities. When you created the opacity mask, a thumbnail appeared to the right of the thumbnail of the artwork that was masked **A**. As in Photoshop, this thumbnail represents your mask. White represents the area of an object that is visible from underneath the mask, and black represents the area that is "knocked out." Areas that are 50 percent black, for instance, will make the object that is being masked have a 50 percent opacity.

The two main settings for opacity masks are Clip and Invert Mask. The Clip option, which is turned on by default, defines the visible area of the opacity mask and the object it is masking. If the Clip option is turned *off* **B**, the masked area is defined by the opacity mask object, but the area around the object is also visible. This means that if artwork goes beyond the object that is defining the opacity mask, the artwork will be visible and will not be affected by the mask, whereas the overlapped area will remain affected by the mask **C**. When the Clip option is turned *on*, the opacity mask object, just like a normal mask, defines the visible area.

The other opacity mask option is Invert Mask **D**, which, as the name implies, reverses the opacity mask effect **E**.

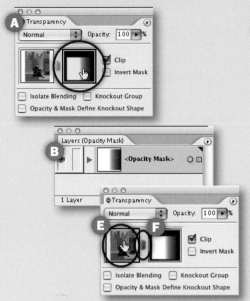

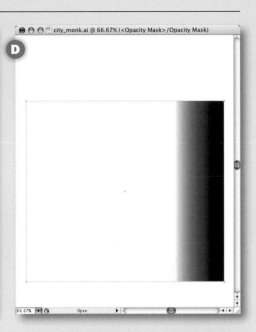

You can modify an opacity mask in two ways. The first option is to select the artwork to which you applied the opacity mask. Then, while selected, click the opacity mask thumbnail in the Transparency palette **A**. This changes the focus from the left-side object thumbnail to the right-side mask thumbnail (as in Photoshop). You'll notice that the layers in the Layers palette have changed, and that they've been replaced by a single opacity mask layer **B**. Don't worry! Your artwork and layers haven't gone anywhere! The changes merely reflect that you are now in a separate "opacity mask mode" where anything you modify, create, or delete affects the opacity mask but nothing else. While in this "mode" you can modify the opacity mask by adding objects (remember to use black and white artwork) or changing the stacking order **C**. The main problem with this option is that while the masked artwork is visible, the opacity mask is invisible, making it difficult to manipulate.

The second option for working with opacity masks is to Option (Alt)-click the mask thumbnail, which will again put you into opacity mask "mode." This time, however, you will see the black and white artwork that composes the opacity mask. With this option you can see exactly how your mask is defined **D**. The downside of this option is that no other artwork is visible, and while you are manipulating the mask you won't have any context on how it is affecting the object(s) it is masking.

To exit opacity mask "mode," click the artwork thumbnail **E** (again, like Photoshop), which brings you back to the regular artboard, making all your layers reappear.

By default, the opacity mask and artwork are locked together, causing the artwork and mask to move together. If you want to move the mask and the artwork independently, unlock the button in the middle of the two thumbnails **F**. 🖰

TIP

Adding to the Opacity Mask Group. Just as with regular masks, it's easy to add to the opacity mask group using Paste in Front/Back, but with one big caveat. Unlike regular masks, you cannot add objects to the opacity mask group if only a single object (not including the opacity mask object) was used in the creation of the opacity mask. To get around this problem, group the single object before you create the opacity mask. It might seem silly to group a single object, but by making that object a group you can add other objects to it by using the Direct Selection tool, clicking on a single path segment or point, and then using Paste in Front/Back. However, you must make sure that only a single point or segment is selected, or you won't be able to paste into the group (this trick also applies to any other group made with a single object).

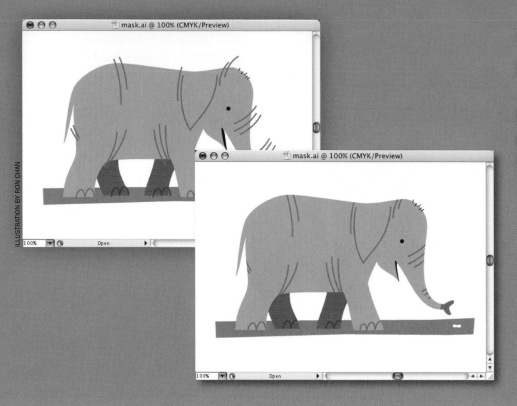

Using Offset Path to Create a Mask

Use Offset Path and Paste in Front/Back to create masks easily.

1. Prepare Your Artwork

Start with the basics. Here we have an illustration of an elephant with line-work to show its "wrinkles." We want to confine the strokes to the body of the elephant but also be able to manipulate the linework later if we need to. You'll do this by masking the linework using the elephant body as the clipping mask. Group the linework first so that it's easy to select at any time. Select one of the strokes and then choose Select > Same > Stroke Color **A**. After all the strokes are selected, they are grouped (Cmd [Ctrl]-G) **B**.

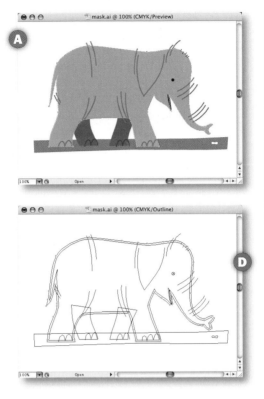

2. Offset the Path

Now for the easy part—making the mask. Really. You first need to create a background element for the clipping mask. You could just make a large rectangle, but by using the existing elephant shape as your starting point, you can create a background shape that conforms to the mask, and in Outline view it will be more easily recognizable than a random rectangle that could very well be part of another object. Select the body of the elephant **A** and choose Object > Path > Offset Path **B**. In the dialog box enter *4* pt **C** to give yourself enough room to "play" with so that the object is easy to select and modify without the clipping mask that you will create later getting in the way. You've now created a slightly larger version of the elephant body that "bleeds" over but is below the stacking order of the shape of the original body **D**.

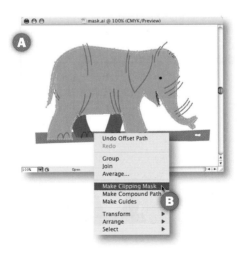

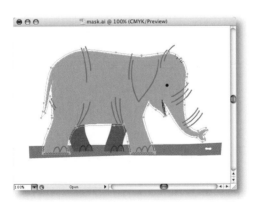

3. Make Your Mask

With the slightly larger version still selected, Shift-click the body so that both the offset path and the original elephant shape are selected **A**. Press Cmd (Ctrl)-7 (Make Clipping Mask) or use the contextual menu **B**, and that's it! You've created a mask with an object below it that has the correct fill with a slight bleed.

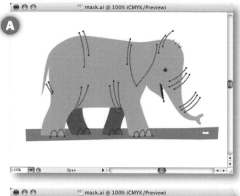

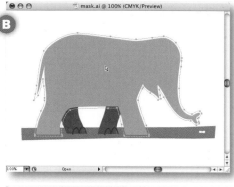

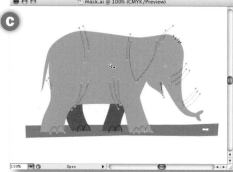

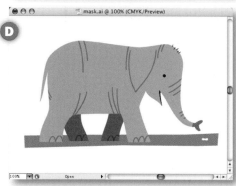

4. Add the Linework

Now add the grouped linework. Just select the linework **A** and cut it to the clipboard. Then use the Direct Select tool and select the elephant body fill you just created **B** and press Cmd (Ctrl)-F to paste the linework in front of the elephant body. The linework is now inside the elephant clipping mask and has the added advantage of being able to be modified or moved at any time using the Direct Selection tool **C**. In the same way you can continually add other objects (such as the tip of the trunk) into the clipping mask using Paste in Front/Back **D**. 🔲

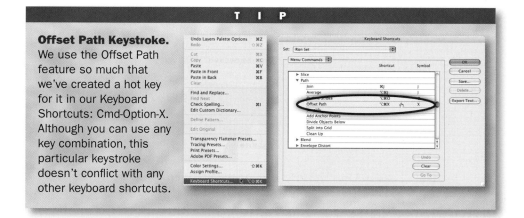

TIP

Offset Path Keystroke.
We use the Offset Path feature so much that we've created a hot key for it in our Keyboard Shortcuts: Cmd-Option-X. Although you can use any key combination, this particular keystroke doesn't conflict with any other keyboard shortcuts.

Blend Theory

Gradients might be easier to create, but not every blend is linear or radial in nature. Here is a way to create blends that conform to any shape you can imagine.

Gradients vs. Blends

A gradient is one of three types of object fill attributes (the others are solid and pattern). However, gradients are either linear (straight) or radial (circular), and it's very difficult to make them appear as though they are following a particular curve or shape. Using the Gradient Mesh tool is one way to create a blend that conforms to a curve or a shape; however, Gradient Mesh is a very difficult, nonintuitive tool to use and is not very accurate. Since you have complete control over the objects that create a blend, they are better suited for irregular shapes and surfaces. Blends can also come in handy if you need to start or stop a gradient at an exact point.

To create a blend, select two objects and then choose Object > Blend > Make or press Cmd (Ctrl)-B. Alternatively, you can create a blend using the Blend tool by clicking anchor points on both objects. Although this can create some fun effects depending on the anchor points you select, most of the time you'll end up using the Blend menu command or shortcut key because it's so much faster.

Top to Bottom

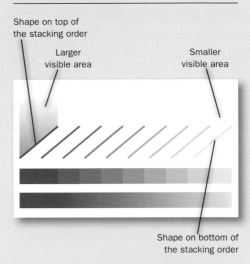

By default, blends graduate objects from top to bottom in the stacking order. This is important to keep in mind because the top object will always show the most "surface area," whereas the bottom object will be partially obscured by the objects on top.

Start and End with the Same Shape

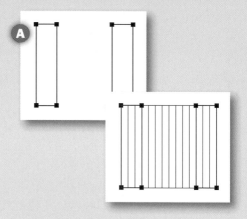

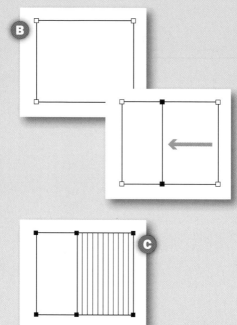

Other Strategies for Shape Blends

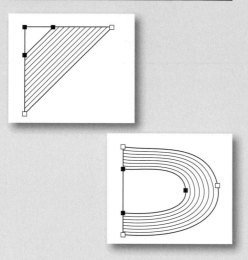

One of the main goals of this book is to enable you to work faster, and what can slow you down more than having to draw the same object twice? When creating a blend, always try to repurpose your objects. There are two ways you can create a blend using the same object.

The first method is to select the object and hold down the Option (Alt) key while dragging the object to the ending position of your blend. Create the blend and you're done **A**.

The second method takes a little more work, but in the end is better in a number of ways. Start by creating an object based on the ending shape of your blend **B**. Using the Selection tool, select the object, and then copy and Paste in Front (Cmd [Ctrl]-C then Cmd [Ctrl]-F). Now,

using the Direct Selection tool, select the anchor point from one side of the object to create a starting point of the blend **C**. Create the blend.

Although both methods produce the same results, blending from a common edge is much cleaner overall than drag-copying the entire object. As your artwork gets more complex you'll appreciate not having the visual distraction, nor the headache, of navigating through extra paths when you work in the Outline view mode.

Here are a couple of examples of shape blend configurations using different types of objects. ▥

ILLUSTRATION BY: RON. CHAN

Blending and Masks

Use blending and clipping masks to render an irregular shape.

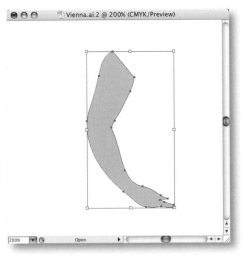

1. Rendering a Statue

Using a combination of blends, offset paths, and clipping masks, we'll render a part of this logo illustration (based on a statue) for a conference in Vienna. The overall figure of the woman was first blocked in with basic objects. Looking at all the objects that need to be rendered can be a little intimidating, so we'll concentrate on one part—the arm of the statue. Select the object that makes up the arm, and then press Cmd-Option (Ctrl-Alt)-Shift-3 to hide all the other objects on the artboard.

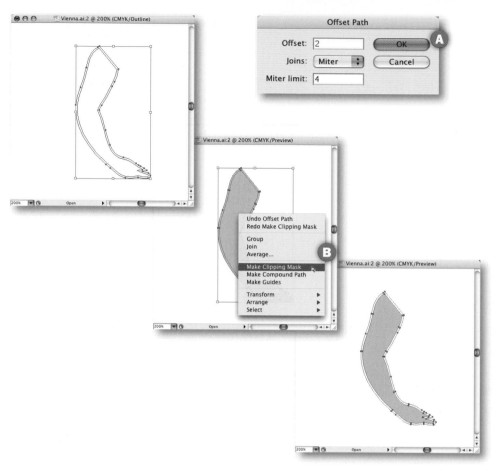

2. Create a Basic Mask

You'll use what you learned earlier in this chapter and create a clipping mask using Offset Path to create a background shape for the mask. With the arm object still selected, choose Object > Path > Offset Path. In the dialog box that appears enter **2** pt and click OK **A**. With the new offset path still selected, hold down the Shift key and select the original shape too. Press Cmd (Ctrl)-7 (or choose Object > Clipping Mask > Make or bring up the contextual menu and choose Make Clipping Mask) to create a mask **B**.

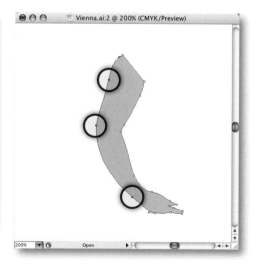

3. Start to Create the Highlight Shape

Using the arm shape as the starting point, create a blend that defines the highlight of the arm. With the Direct Selection tool, select the left side anchor points of the arm shape (now being used as a clipping mask). Press Cmd (Ctrl)-C to copy the path segment, and then press Cmd (Ctrl)-F to paste the segment on top of the mask in the exact same location.

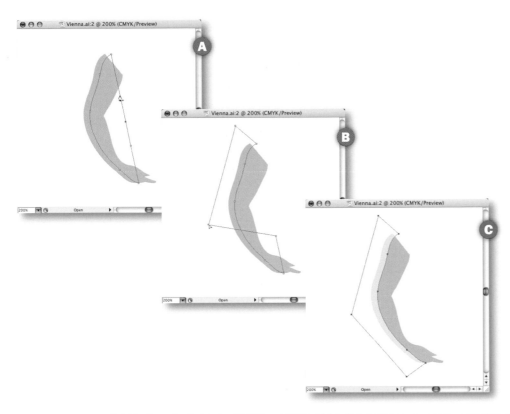

4. Finish Creating the Highlight Shape

Now move the path segment with the Selection tool to the point where the highlight will end. With the path segment still selected, press Cmd (Ctrl)-J to close the path. Use the Add Anchor Point tool to add three anchor points to the newly enclosed path **A**. Using the new anchor points, create a shape that extends past the arm **B**. Then fill the new shape with a highlight color. You'll see that the highlight shape conforms to the contour of the arm and sits inside the clipping mask **C**.

5. Rule Breaker: The Shape Becomes Part of the Mask

Since the shape you just created was taken from a segment of the clipping mask and then *pasted in front* of that same clipping mask, based on the rule about masks always needing to be on the top layer in the stacking order, why did the highlight shape become part of the clipping mask? Unfortunately, explaining the inner workings of why masks work in this way is beyond the scope of this book or project. Suffice it to say that a) it works, and b) if you really need a detailed explanation of *why* it works, check out Mordy Golding's Illustrator blog site at *http://rwillustrator.blogspot.com/2006/08/ask-mordy-you-gotta-read-between-lines.html* where his mission in life is to explain Illustrator's many unsolved mysteries.

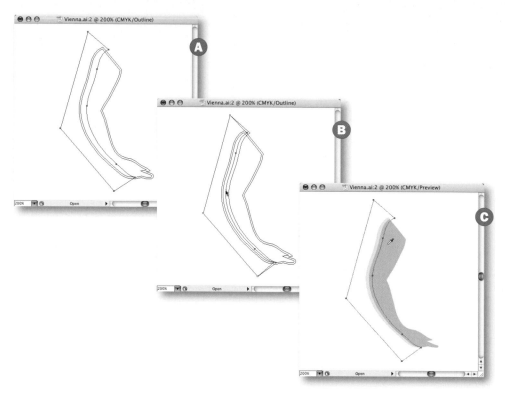

6. Make the Starting Point of the Highlight

Now, back to the show...Select the highlight shape you just created and press Cmd (Ctrl)-C to copy the shape and then Cmd (Ctrl)-F to paste the copy in front of the original shape **A**. Using the Direct Selection tool, select the anchor points that make up the curve and move that portion of the curve to the starting point of the blend **B**. Fill the original highlight shape with the body color **C**.

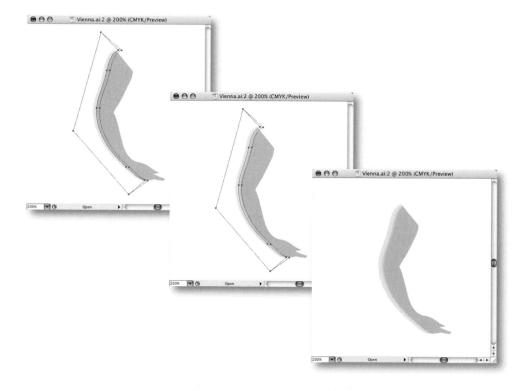

7. Create the Blend

Create the blend of the two shadow shapes by selecting both shapes and then pressing Cmd-Option (Ctrl-Alt)-B (or choose Object > Blend > Make). The result is a blended shadow that conforms to the shape of the arm. ▥

Using Opacity Masks to Create Gradients on Gradients

Create gradient "swoops" that blend into other gradients.

ILLUSTRATION BY RON CHAN

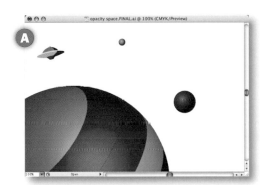

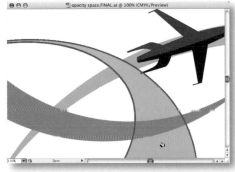

1. Create the Base Artwork

One of the hardest effects to achieve in Illustrator has always been to create a gradient that intersects another gradient. Although this effect can easily be done in Photoshop using layer masks, the downside is that the artwork isn't scalable because it's raster-based. The problem with an Illustrator gradient is that it must have a "starting" color and an "ending" color. A gradient cannot start or end with a value of "no fill," and consequently the gradient must blend into a solid background color. With the introduction of opacity masks this "blend on blend" is not only easy to achieve but very flexible too.

In this project we'll create a series of solid colored "swoops" that overlap and interact with each other, and with background gradients and rendered spheres as well. But first we need to create the basic artwork including the "striped" planet and flying saucer (see Chapter 2, "Create 3D Planets") **A**. For the "swoops" we'll use two overlapping circles and Live Paint to give us the greatest flexibility. **B**

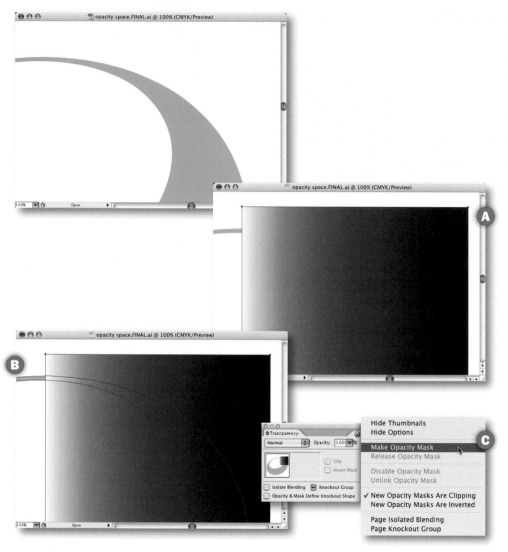

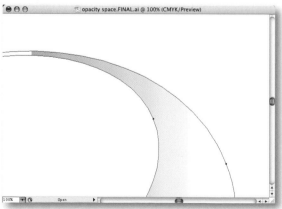

2. Create the Opacity Mask

Draw a rectangle on top of one of the swoops. Fill the rectangle with a simple black and white gradient **A**. Remember, although you can create an opacity mask with any color, it's preferable to use black and white.

After making the gradient, select both the gradient and the swoop **B**, go to the Transparency palette and in the palette menu choose Make Opacity Mask **C**.

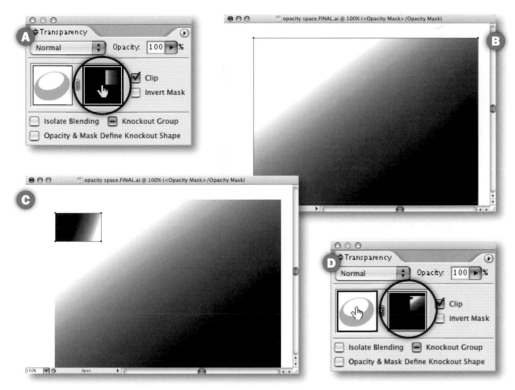

3. Tweak the Opacity Mask

In the Transparency palette either click or Option (Alt)-click the opacity mask thumbnail **A** to modify the gradient so that there is a nice transition from the lower left corner to 3/4 of the way toward the rocket ship **B**. Then create another gradient at the opposite end of the swoop to make it fade off at the end of the rocket **C**. When you're done, click the artwork thumbnail **D** to go back to the regular artwork mode. The result should be a gradient that fades off on both ends to no fill while also showing the background planet gradients behind it **E**.

Repeat the preceding steps as many times as you like, and then position the swoops in front or in back of each other by changing the stacking order **F**.

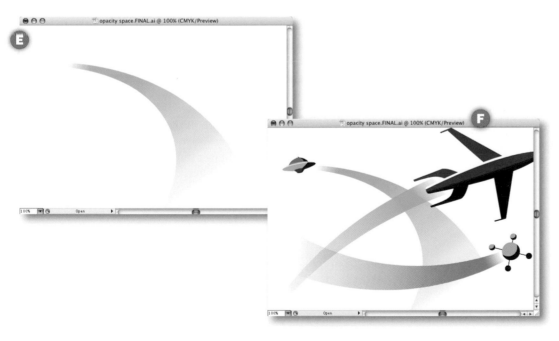

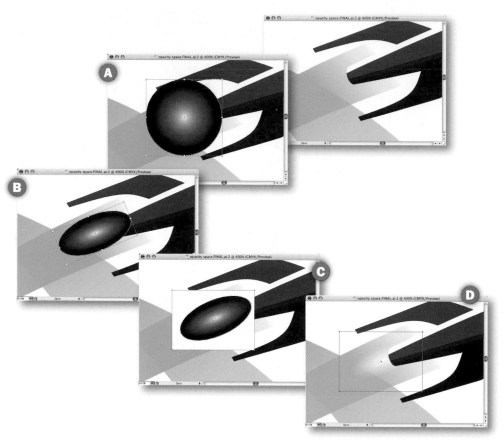

4. Make the Rocket Engine Blast

Create the "blast" coming from the rocket's engine with another opacity mask. Draw a circle and fill it with a Radial Gradient from white in the center to black at the outer edge **A**. Using the Free Transform tool or Selection tool bounding box, squeeze the circle so that the gradient "flattens" out a bit **B**. Now create a simple white rectangle and cut and paste in back of the gradient you just made. Select them both and create an opacity mask from the two objects **C**. The result is a graduated white "blast" that fades to nothing at the edges. All that's left to do is to cut and paste the blast in back of the rocket and move it into position **D**.

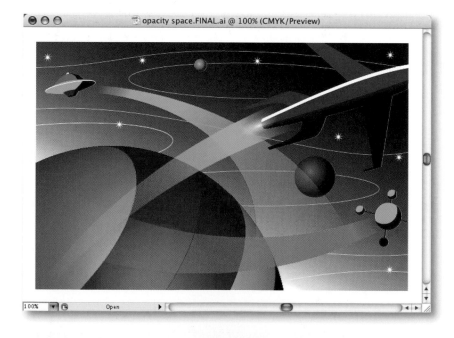

5. Add the Final Touches

To complete the image, drop a gradient fill into the background, bring back the other artwork, and then add some final touches such as stars, spatial anomalies, and so on. ▥

Masks Within Masks

Use the stacking technique of Paste in Front/Back to create a clipping mask within a clipping mask.

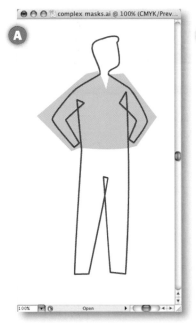

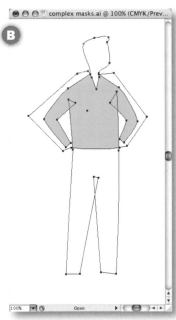

1. Create a Basic Mask

The goal of this project is to create a shirt that will be confined to the shape of a body using a clipping mask, and then create a pattern that is confined to the shirt using another clipping mask.

Create the basic figure shape, and then create an object in the shape of a shirt **A**. Use the Selection tool to select the shirt, and then cut the shirt object to the clipboard. Select the body object and paste the shirt object on the clipboard behind the body (Cmd [Ctrl]-B). Select both objects and create a clipping mask by pressing Cmd (Ctrl)-7 or choose Object > Clipping Mask > Make (or you can use the contextual menu and choose Make Clipping Mask) **B**.

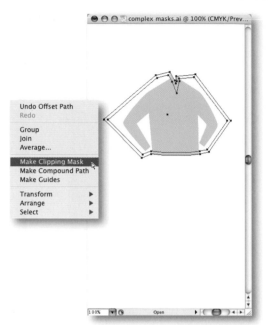

2. Create the Shirt Mask

Select the shirt object by holding down the Option (Alt) key while clicking with the Direct Selection tool to select the entire shirt (remember, when a mask is made, it groups the objects together so you'll need to direct select the shirt) and create an Offset Path of *2* pt (choose Object > Path > Offset Path). With the offset path object you just made still selected, Shift-click the original shirt object and create a clipping mask (Cmd [Ctrl]-7). You've just made a mask within a mask!

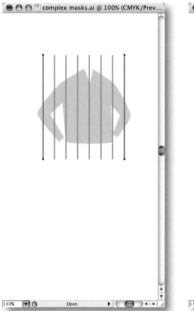

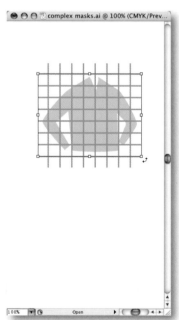

3. Create a Pattern

Create a simple checkerboard pattern by drawing a single stroke on top of the shirt. Option (Alt)-drag (creating a copy) the stroke to the other side of the shirt. Select both strokes and blend them (Cmd-Option [Ctrl-Alt]-B). Double-click the Blend tool in the Tools palette to bring up the Blend dialog box. In the Specified Steps option, modify the number of steps to *6*, and then click OK. Select the strokes (which include the blend) and copy and paste in front. With the strokes you just pasted still selected, rotate them 90 degrees.

4. Put the Pattern into the Mask

Select the whole pattern and cut it to the clipboard. With the Direct Selection tool, select the shirt background object **A** (the offset path shirt object you made earlier) and paste the pattern in front (Cmd [Ctrl]-F) **B**.

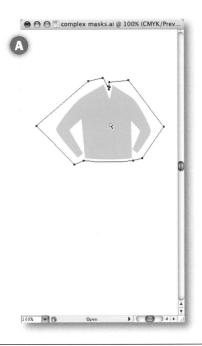

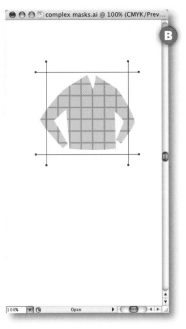

5. Fill in the Rest of the Figure

We drew the pants, skin, hair, and belt shapes (shown here as if the shapes weren't confined to the body clipping mask **A**) and then used Paste in Front/Back to drop them into the correct stacking order inside the body clipping mask. The other details **B** were placed on top of the body clipping mask.

Shadows were added to the shirt by creating shapes and pasting them in front of the shirt pattern. We then applied a Multiply blend mode and an Opacity of 80% to the shadow in the Transparency palette **C**.

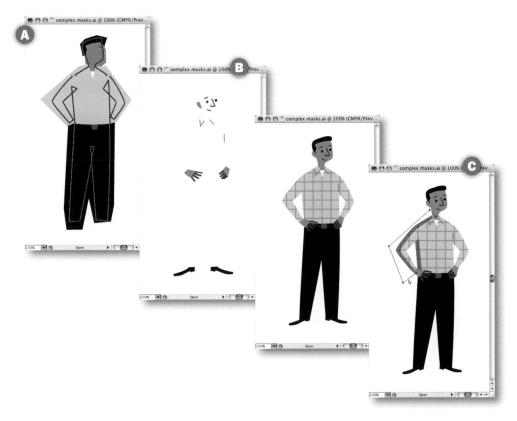

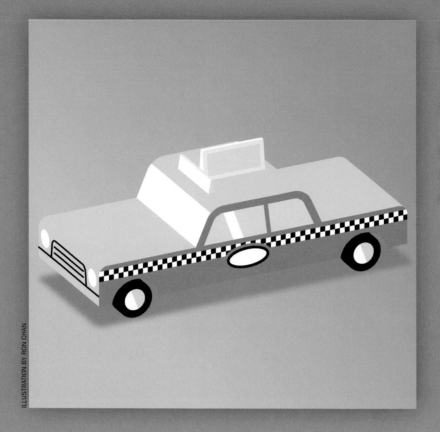

Create a Transparent Shadow

Use Gaussian Blur to create a soft-edged shadow against a graduated background.

Round Corners

Radius: 5 pt   OK **A**

Cancel

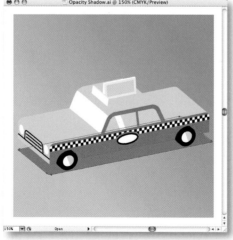

T I P

Creating a Shadow Color. You can create a darker "shadow" color in many ways. Since colors are so subjective, there really is no "right" way. Try our method. Start with the base color, go to the Color palette (in CMYK mode) and while holding down the Shift key move any color slider to the right (darker) about 10%. In the K (black) field increase the intensity to between 25–40%.

1. Create the Shadow

Creating a soft-edged effect using Gaussian Blur is as easy to do in Illustrator as it is in Photoshop—well, almost. In this example we'll add a soft-edged shadow under the taxi.

Create a rectangle to use as the shape of the shadow. Cut the shadow rectangle (Cmd [Ctrl]-X), then select the blue gradient background and press Cmd (Ctrl)-F to paste the shadow in front. Round the edges of the rectangle to make the corners softer by selecting the shadow rectangle and choosing Filter > Stylize > Round Corners. When the Round Corners dialog box appears enter *5* pt and click OK **A**.

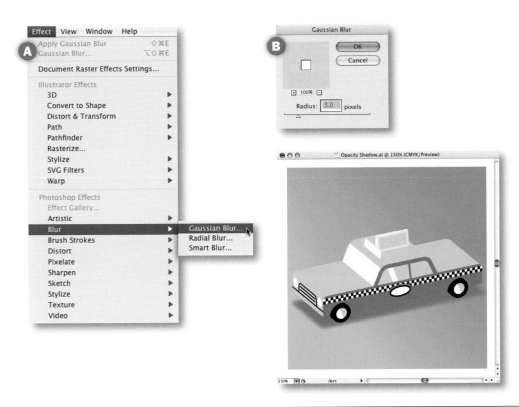

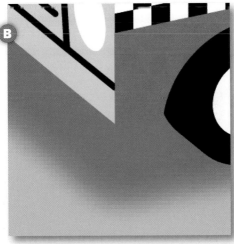

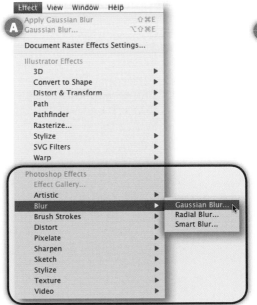

Gaussian Blur radius: 3 pixels; 72 ppi

2. Use Gaussian Blur

With the shadow still selected, choose Effect > Blur > Gaussian Blur **A**. In the dialog box enter *3* for the pixel radius **B**. You've just created a beautiful soft-edged shadow that blends perfectly into the background—but there's one big, fat caveat!...

3. Photoshop Effects = Resolution

When you chose the Gaussian Blur effect, you might not have noticed that the effect was in the Photoshop Effects category **A**. Using Photoshop Effects requires that you think in pixels, not in vectors. Your first clue should have been when you entered a value in *pixels*, not in *points* or *inches*, in the Gaussian Blur dialog box. Since Illustrator is a vector-based application, you usually don't have to worry about resolution, but since Gaussian Blur is a pixel-based filter, just as in Photoshop, you need to make sure that the resolution (the number of pixels in your file) is correct for the final output of your file.

Zooming in you'll see that the beautiful soft-edged shadow is actually very pixilated **B**—just like the pixilation that occurs when you zoom in on a 72 pixels

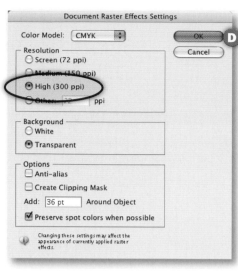

per inch (*ppi*), or computer screen resolution, file in Photoshop. Because the effect is pixel-based and the resolution is set by default to 72 ppi (see "Caution: 72 dpi by Default"), the soft edge will *only* look good at 100 percent on your computer screen or on the Web.

Select Effect > Document Raster Effects Settings **C** and in the dialog box that appears change the resolution to **300** ppi and click OK **D**. Since the resolution is now set higher, and there are 300 pixels per inch instead of 72, the 3-pixel blur distance we originally specified is much narrower than we would like **E**.

Gaussian Blur radius: 3 pixels; 300 ppi

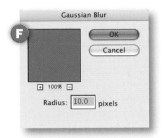

With the shadow selected, go to the Appearance palette and double-click the Gaussian Blur layer to bring up the Gaussian Blur dialog box again **F**.

This time enter *10* for the pixel radius. Click OK and you'll see that the shadow looks great again and that setting the resolution when using Photoshop Effects can make a big difference **G**. ▥

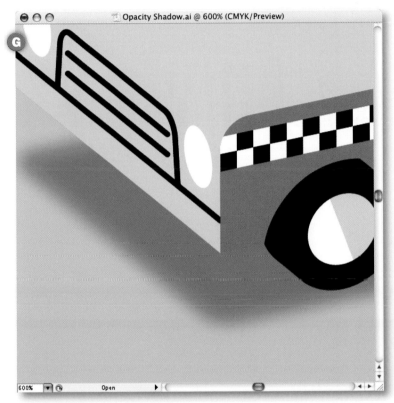

Gaussian Blur radius: 10 pixels; 300 ppi

4

BEING CREATIVE WITH BRUSHES AND PATTERNS

Using Strokes, Brushes, and Patterns to Outline and Fill Your Paths and Objects

GET INNOVATIVE WITH STROKES *122*

UNLEASH THE POTENTIAL OF THE ART BRUSH *126*

CREATE A TEXTURED STROKE FROM AN ART BRUSH *130*

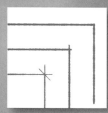

MAKE A TEXTURED STROKE WITH A SCATTER BRUSH *132*

MAKE A CHECKERBOARD OR GINGHAM *134*

CREATE A QUILT PATTERN *140*

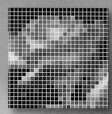

CREATE A MOSAIC FOR A TILE PROJECT *143*

WHILE THERE IS SOMETHING to be said for the purity of crisp, clean lines and solid, colored fills, one could also argue the merits of textures and patterns for breathing some life into sometimes staid digital illustrations. The aim of this chapter is to tickle your creative juices by showing you a handful of possibilities that exist with strokes, brushes, and patterns. We hope you'll take it from there and create your own fabulous art using these Illustrator tools.

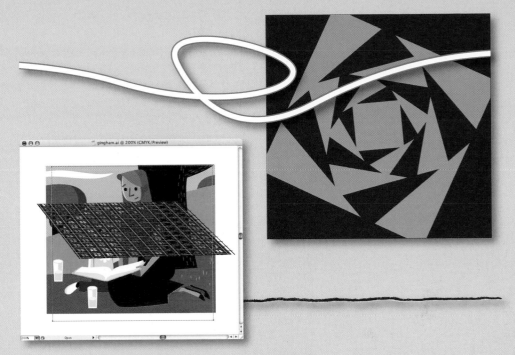

Strokes

Although most of your artwork likely has simple, thin solid lines—or no strokes at all—the strokes we show here can be used for accents like borders or as the occasional embellishment, such as a shoelace or necklace. Why use a stroke for these elements instead of drawing them? In the long run it's quicker to produce and edit strokes, leaving you more time for working with the meat of your illustration.

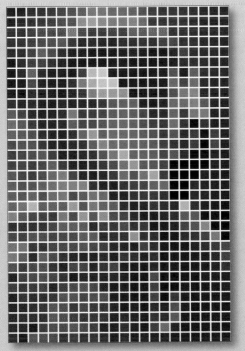

Brushes

The world of brushes is vast, and we don't propose to show the thousands of ways you can create and use the various types of brushes Illustrator offers. Instead, we show you a few ways in whch working illustrators are using brushes to give their artwork a unique style or make their digital art look more organic and handcrafted.

Patterns

Creating a basic pattern is an easy task in Illustrator, but unless you're a textile designer, trying to find practical uses for patterns is sometimes harder. We'll show you a couple of projects on how to create patterns you may be able to use in your illustrations, such as stripes and checkerboards. Finally, for the handy folks out there, we'll also provide a couple of fun tips on how to use Illustrator to create patterns for quilts and tile projects.

Get Innovative with Strokes

Paths, or the outlines of objects, can take on a life beyond the mundane solid line. By using dashed strokes, layered strokes, and multiple strokes, you can easily create a variety of looks and styles. An added bonus? Strokes are quicker to make and edit than shapes.

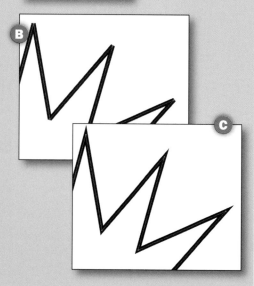

Looking at the Stroke Palette

The Stroke palette is command central when it comes to defining the look of your stroke. In the palette you'll find stroke attributes such as weight, miter limit, caps and joins, alignment to the stroke, and dashed options. To change the attributes of any stroke, simply select the path or object and change, or select, your desired value or option. Here is a rundown of each of these attributes **A**:

- **Weight:** The weight of a stroke is how thick or thin it is. You can enter a value between 0 and 1000 pt to determine the thickness of a stroke.

- **Miter Limit:** When you select a Miter Join, you can enter a miter limit value between 1 and 500 pt. The miter limit determines how pointy your joins can get before Illustrator bevels, or squares, them off. This avoids points that look abnormally long. A miter limit of 1 bevels all points, whereas a value of 500 won't bevel anything except extremely acute angles. In the figure, the 4 pt star on the top left has a miter limit of 2 **B**, and the figure on the bottom right has a miter limit of 5 **C**.

- **Align Stroke:** If your path is closed (as with a shape), you can choose how to align your stroke along the path. Choose from Align Stroke To Center, To Inside, or To Outside.

- **Caps:** A cap is the end of an open path. Choose from Butt (squared end), Round (rounded end), or Projecting (squared end that extends half the width of the line beyond the end).

- **Joins:** Essentially a corner, a join is formed when a straight path changes direction. Choose from Miter (pointed corner), Round (rounded corner), or Bevel (squared corner).

- **Dashed Line:** Select this option to create a dashed line.

- **Dash/Gap:** Enter two to six values to create the pattern of your dashed stroke. For more details see the following section, "Dashed Strokes."

T I P

Changing the Color of a Stroke. To change the color of a stroke, select the Stroke box in the toolbox. Then select your path or object and choose a color from the Color or Swatches palette. You may also drag the color from the Stroke box onto any path or object, whether or not it is selected. To quickly toggle between having the fill or stroke active in the toolbox, press the X key.

T I P

Selecting a Stroke in a Live Paint Group. To select the stroke of an individual object within a Live Paint group, use the Live Paint Selection tool rather than the regular Selection tool. Otherwise, you'll select all of the edges of the group.

Dashed Strokes

To create a dashed stroke you must specify the length of the dash and then the length of the gap between the dashes. The dash and gap represent the visible and transparent areas of the stroke, respectively. As we mentioned earlier, you can use as little as one value (Illustrator will use the same value for the dash and gap) for simple strokes and up to six values for more complex strokes. You can create strokes with even and consistent dashes and gaps or strokes that vary in size and spacing.

How do you know what values to use? You can find numerous tips online. Or, you can always try good ol' experimentation. If neither of those options appeals to you, here is a table of some time-tested strokes to get you started. Just draw a straight line with the Pen tool and set your Fill to None.

	Weight in Points	End Cap	Dash/Gap
A	3	round	0/6
B	4	butt	4/4
C	10	butt	4/3
D	4	round	2/10/10/10
E	6	round	12/0/12/0/12

Expanding Strokes

If you want to expand a stroke into a filled object, choose Object > Path > Outline Stroke. If you want to color, rotate, or otherwise manipulate the individual dashes of a dashed line, you must convert the stroke into a series of individual objects. Here are the few steps you need to execute this "trick":

1. Select the stroke and choose Object > Flatten Transparency **A**. In the Flatten Transparency dialog box, set the Raster/Vector Balance to *100* and select Convert All Strokes to Outlines.

2. Choose Object > Compound Paths > Release **B**.

3. Choose Object > Ungroup.

4. Select the individual dashed object and color or transform to your liking **C**.

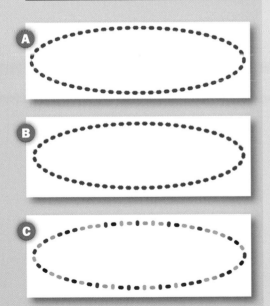

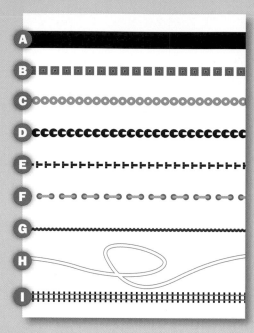

Layered Strokes

To create more complex strokes, you can create more than one path and stack them over one another. Create the first path, select it, and choose Edit > Copy and Edit > Paste In Front. Create a second layer and move the copied path onto that layer by dragging the Selected Art indicator (small blue square) in the Layers palette. Format as desired. Repeat for additional paths.

	Line	Points	Color*	End Cap	Dash/Gap
A	1	20	black	butt	solid (uncheck dashed)
	2	15	white	butt	3/5
	3	10	black	butt	solid
B	1	10	any	projecting	0/13.5
	2	5	white	projecting	0/13.5
	3	2.5	any	projecting	0/13.5
C	1	10	any	round	0/10
	2	5	white	round	0/10
D	1	10	any	round	0/10
	2	5	white	butt	5/5
E	1	7.5	any	butt	2.5/7.5
	2	5	same as 1	butt	5/5
	3	2.5	same as 1	butt	7.5/2.5
F	1	7	any @100%	round	0/14/0/12
	2	4	same as 1 @50%	round	14/12
G	1	5	any	round	0/4.5
	2	5	white	round	0/4.5 offset
H	1	4.5	any	butt	solid
	2	3	white	butt	solid
I	1	12	black	butt	2/4
	2	7	black	butt	solid
	3	6	white	butt	solid
	4	5	black	butt	solid
	5	4	white	butt	solid
	6	4	black	butt	2/4

*choose any color unless otherwise indicated

Multiple Strokes

You can also use the Appearance palette to create multiple strokes within the same path or object. Many of the stroke effects mentioned in the previous section can also be achieved via using multiple strokes and the Appearance palette. While the Appearance palette may be a little more complex than the Layers palette, its advantage is that you can edit your strokes to get them exactly the way you want them to look quickly and easily.

To create multiple strokes, follow these steps:

1. Select your path or object. You can also target a path in the Layers palette (select the target circle).

2. From the Appearance palette menu, choose Add New Stroke.

3. Select your desired color. Also select your stroke weight, joins, caps, and dashed options in the Stroke palette.

4. Repeat steps 2 and 3 as necessary. If you feel the need to tweak any strokes, you can always edit the stroke attributes by simply selecting the stroke in the Appearance palette and changing any attribute.

Note that just as you can shuffle layers in the Layers palette, you can also rearrange the order of the multiple strokes in the Appearance palette. ▥

Saving as a Graphic Style. If you really like the multiple stroke you've created, save it as a Graphic Style. That way you can quickly apply the look of the multiple stroke to any path or object, and even text. Simply select your stroke and click the New Graphic Style button in the Graphic Styles palette.

T I P

ILLUSTRATION BY BRYAN LEISTER

Unleash the Potential of the Art Brush

Exploit the potential of custom brushes using world-renowned illustrator Bryan Leister's novel approach. Bryan can produce figures with endless variations using just six paths.

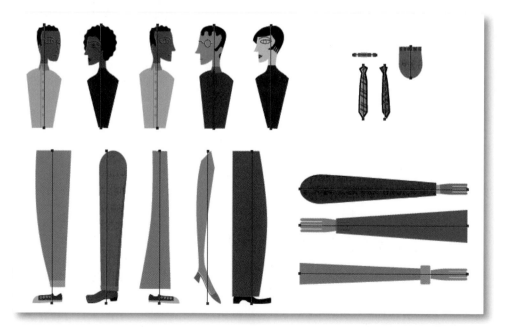

1. Create the Body Parts

Unquestionably, creating body parts is the hardest part of this project and, of course, will depend on your illustrative prowess. This task is meant to serve as inspiration for whatever your imagination can come up with. In this example, Bryan has created five basic body parts for his library with numerous variations of each. Shown here are torsos, legs, arms, neckties, and belts.

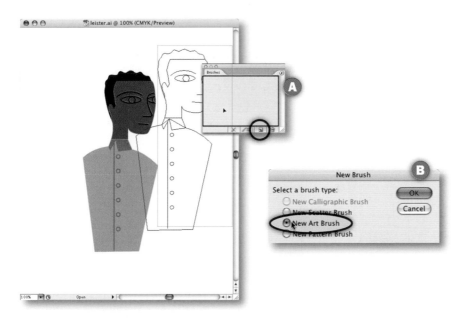

2. Create the Torso

We'll focus on creating a new Art Brush from the torso artwork by selecting the art and either dragging it into the Brushes palette or clicking the New Brush button at the bottom of the palette **A**. Choose New Art Brush from the New Brush dialog box and click OK **B**. The Art Brush Options dialog box appears.

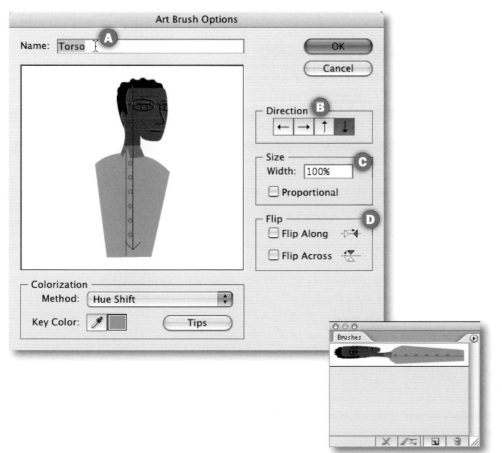

3. Art Brush Options

In the Art Brush Options dialog box you can specify the following:

A *Art Brush Name:* Although it's tempting to just use the default name, in this case since you know that you will be specifying quite a few brushes, it's a good idea to organize your brushes by giving them identifiable (or meaningful) names instead of just using "Art Brush 52."

B *Direction:* The Direction setting specifies the orientation of the artwork in relation to the path the Art Brush is applied to.

C *Size:* The Width option adjusts the width of the artwork relative to the artwork's original width. By selecting the Proportional box, the artwork will be scaled in proportion. In this exercise the width is set to 100%, but Proportional is *not* selected.

D *Flip:* The Flip option changes the orientation of the artwork on the vertical or horizontal axis in relation to the path in much the same way as the Reflect tool does.

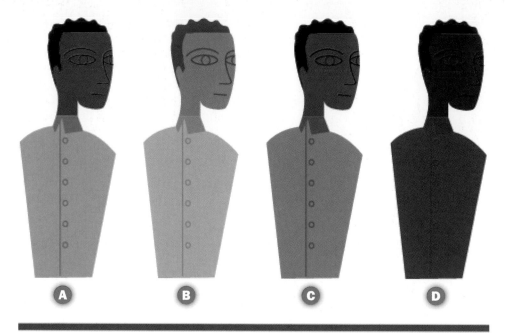

Stroke color

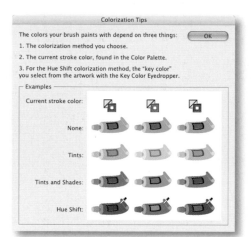

T I P

Colorization Guide. You can find a handy guide to how Colorization can affect your Art Brush by clicking the Tips button at the bottom of the Art Brush Options dialog box.

4. Colorization Options

The last Art Brush Option in the dialog box (see previous page) is Colorization. Depending on which option you choose, this option determines how the brush artwork is affected by the stroke color of the path. Here are the Colorization choices:

A *None:* Choosing None disregards the stroke color and renders the artwork with the same colors it had when originally made into an Art Brush.

B *Tints:* Tints displays your brush artwork in tints of the stroke color. The black portions of your artwork will display as 100% of the stroke color. The whites in your artwork will remain white. Any tones in between will display as tint percentages of your stroke color. Tints are used mainly for black and white artwork.

C *Tints and Shades:* This option is similar to Tints except that Tints and Shades maintains black as a color throughout the Art Brush artwork. Choose Tints and Shades for grayscale artwork for the most predictable results.

D *Hue Shift:* Hue Shift uses the color in the Key Color box. Everything in your brush artwork that has the key color displays in the stroke color of the path. The other colors in the artwork display as colors related to the stroke color. Hue Shift maintains black, white, and gray. By default, the key color is the predominant color in your Art Brush artwork. To change the key color, click the Eyedropper icon in the dialog box and then click any part of the artwork in the preview pane of the Art Brush Options dialog box. Choose Hue Shift if your artwork contains multiple colors.

For our torso Art Brush we chose the Hue Shift Colorization method.

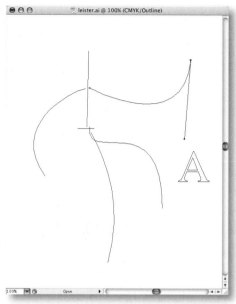

5. Create the Figure

After converting all the body parts of the figure into Art Brushes, draw six paths and assign one of the Art Brushes you made to each path. Adjust the ends of the strokes to connect to the other body parts and you've created a fully poseable figure. ▦

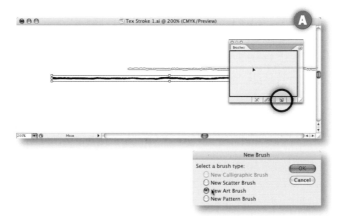

Create a Textured Stroke from an Art Brush

Tired of the crisp perfection of vector art? Use textured strokes to give the appearance of hand-drawn artwork.

1. Place a Scan of a Pencil Stroke into Illustrator

Our first step was to draw (yes, hand draw!) a single 3-inch line with a pencil on a piece of paper **A**. We scanned in our glorious piece of artwork and cleaned it up a little in Photoshop before placing it into Illustrator where we used Live Trace **B** to create a vector path from the scan (see "Convert Engravings into Line Art with Live Trace" in Chapter 2, "Freeform Drawing and Geometric Shapes," for more details on how to work with Live Trace) **C**.

2. Create a New Art Brush

Expand the Live Trace artwork (Object > Live Trace > Expand). Next, make sure that any white areas are deleted by choosing Select > Same > Fill Color to select all of the white areas, and then delete them. (For more on the Select Same feature, see "Select Same Strategies" in Chapter 2.) Create a new Art Brush by selecting the object you just created and dragging it into the Brushes palette or click the New Brush button at the bottom of the palette **A**. For a detailed explanation of the Art Brush Options settings, see "Unleash the

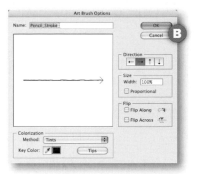

Potential of the Art Brush" earlier in this chapter.

For this textured stroke, enter **100%** in the Size setting (it's 100% by default) and clear the Proportional option. Since this is black and white artwork, select Tints as the Colorization method. Name the stroke "Pencil_Stroke" and then click OK to create the stroke **B**.

3. Apply the Art Brush

Using artwork that previously included normal solid strokes **A**, we applied our "Pencil_Stroke" by selecting the paths and then clicking the thumbnail of the Pencil_Stroke in the Brushes palette. To make your brush appear thicker or thinner, go to the Stroke palette and increase or decrease the stroke weight. In this instance, give the strokes with the Pencil_Stroke Art Brush a weight of *.75 pt* **B**.

Using an Art Brush like the Pencil_ Stroke in combination with a filled object can give the edge of your object a little more of hand-drawn look **C**.

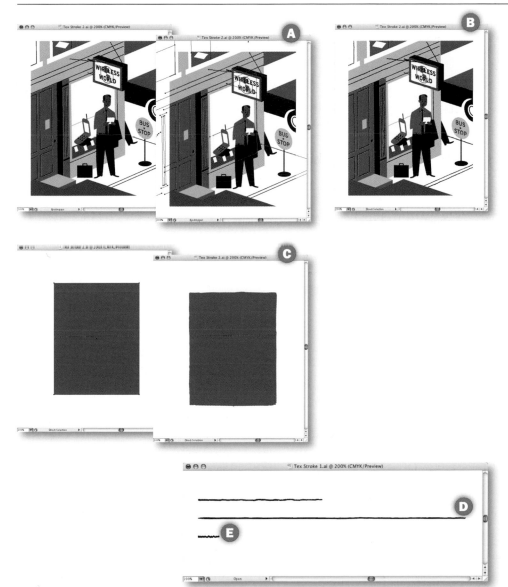

The downside to using an Art Brush for a stroke is that the appearance of the textured stroke depends greatly on the length of the path to which the Art Brush is applied. A long path will stretch the appearance of the Art Brush **D**, whereas a short path will squeeze it like an accordion **E**. One option is to create Art Brushes of varying lengths. For longer paths, another option is to cut up the path so that the Art Brush won't have to stretch so far.

If you decide that you want more consistency in your texture appearance on longer path lengths, you might get better results if you use a Scatter Brush, as explained in the next section. 🖐

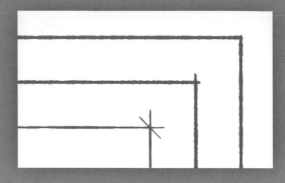

Make a Textured Stroke with a Scatter Brush

Simulate a hand-drawn texture with a Scatter Brush.

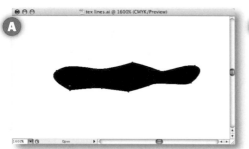

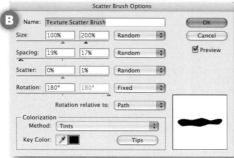

1. Create a Scatter Brush

Start with a very simple object **A** to create another type of textured stroke, this time using the Scatter Brush. Create a small rounded shape, and from that artwork make a Scatter Brush (for more on how to create a Scatter Brush see "Use the Scatter Brush to Make a Texture" in the Supplement). Enter a Size setting of *100%* to *200%*, a Spacing setting of *19%* to *17%*, and a Scatter setting of *0%* to *1%*. For the Colorization method, choose Tints **B**.

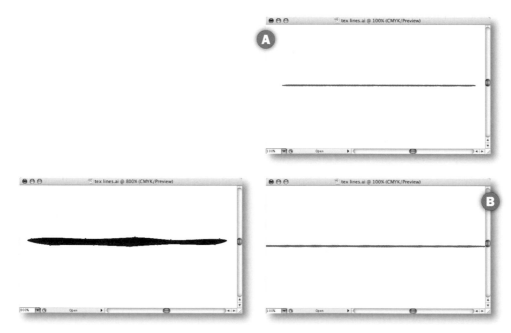

2. Use the Textured Scatter Brush

Using your new textured Scatter Brush on a long path will produce a more consistent, not stretched, appearance **A**. By horizontally scaling the original artwork and creating another Scatter Brush, you can see that the appearance is a little smoother because there are not as many instances of the Scatter Brush artwork **B**.

However, a problem arises when using a Scatter Brush in this way when the path turns a corner. One instance of the Scatter Brush artwork sits on the tip of the

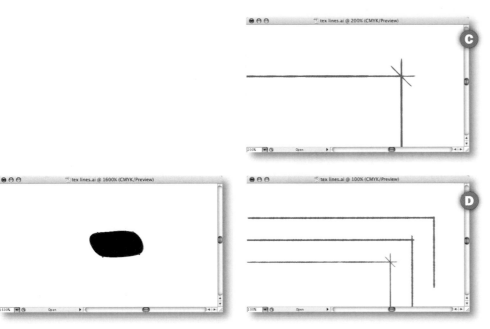

corner, not conforming to the direction of the path **C**.

To solve the problem of a Scatter Brush artwork instance displaying oddly on the corner you can either divide the path into sections so that it doesn't have a corner or create a Scatter Brush that uses artwork whose width and height are approximately equal. Shown here are three copies of the same path, each with a different brush applied. The top path uses a brush created from a shorter piece of artwork (seen at far left) and consequently turns the corner well. The bottom two paths use brushes made of progressively longer pieces of artwork, which creates problems at the corner **D**. 🖐

T I P

Creating Your Own Set of Brushes.
Just as important as creating a set of brushes is having them available to use from any Illustrator document. Create the brushes that you need in the ways described in this chapter. Then, from the Brushes palette menu, choose Save Brush Library and give your library a name. The library is automatically stored in the Brushes folder (Presets > Brushes) **A**. The next time you launch Illustrator your brush set will appear when you choose Open Brush Library from the Brushes palette menu **B**. If you want your custom brushes library to always be present in Illustrator, choose "Persistent" from the custom library's palette menu **C**.

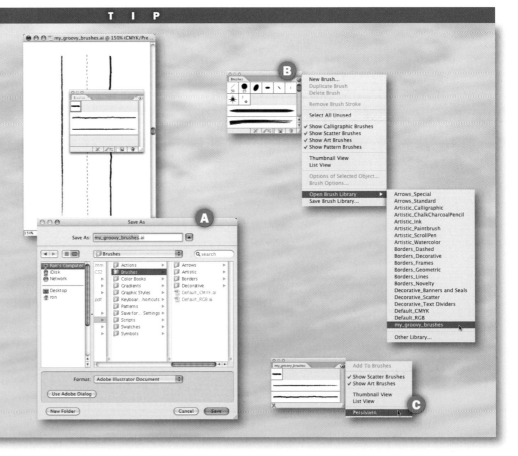

ILLUSTRATION BY RON CHAN

Make a Checkerboard or Gingham

Use blends, transparency, selection tools, and even 3D to create a pattern for a picnic cloth.

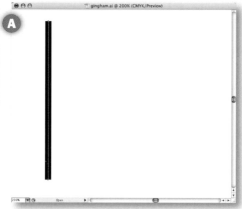

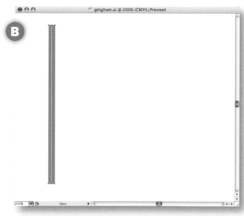

1. Create the Basic Stripes

To create a gingham pattern to use as the cloth for this picnic scene, you first need to create a single path with a 10 pt stroke **A**. Apply a blue color to the stroke. Copy the path and press Cmd (Ctrl)-B to paste a copy of the path in back of the original, and with the copy of the path still selected press Cmd-Option (Ctrl-Alt)-O to outline the stroke. Click the original path (in front of the outlined stroke that you just created) and change it to a 1 pt white stroke **B**.

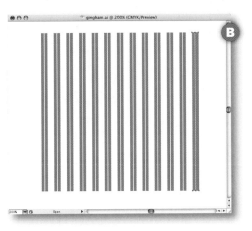

2. Duplicate the Stroke

Now go to the Preferences dialog box (Cmd [Ctrl]-K), and with the unit of measure set to points, enter **20** in the Keyboard Increment field **A**. Since the main stripe is 10 pt, a 20 pt distance will give you a gap of 10 pt—or the width of one stripe. Select both the 1 pt stroke and the stripe, and then press Option (Alt)-right arrow 11 times to create 12 duplicates **B**.

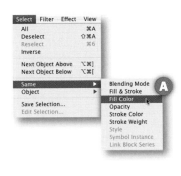

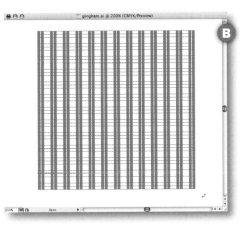

3. Rotate the Objects

Select one of the blue stripes and choose Select > Same > Fill Color to select all the blue stripes **A**. Now Group all of the blue stripes (Cmd [Ctrl]-G). Select all the objects, press Cmd (Ctrl)-C, and then press Cmd (Ctrl)-F (Copy and Paste in Front) to create a duplicate of the objects. With the pasted objects still selected, use either the Free Transform tool (press the E key) or the Selection tool to rotate the copy 90 degrees **B**.

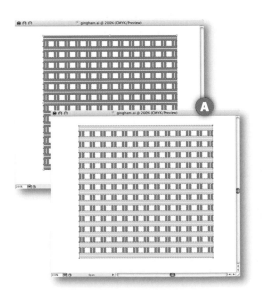

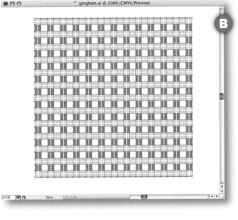

4. Stack the Stripes

With the Selection tool, select the horizontal blue stripes and change the color to green **A**. Select and cut (Cmd [Ctrl]-X) the green and blue stripes to the clipboard. Now select all the white strokes (Cmd [Ctrl]-A) and group them (Cmd [Ctrl]-G). With the strokes still selected, paste the stripes in the clipboard in back of the white strokes (Cmd [Ctrl]-B) **B**.

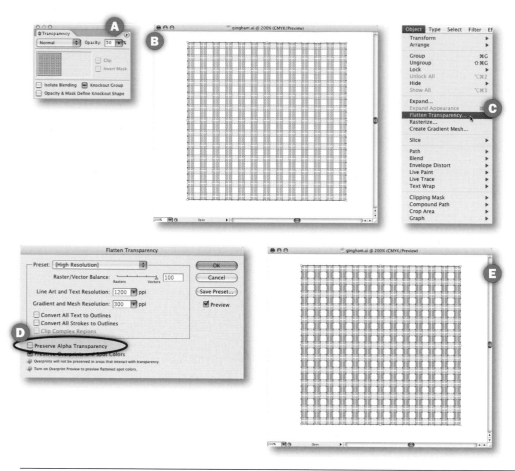

5. Make the Stripes Overlap

With the stripes still selected go to the Transparency palette and give the stripes an Opacity setting of **50%** **A**. You'll see that in the sections where the stripes overlap there is a change in color due to the transparency **B**. Now, with stripes still selected choose Object > Flatten Transparency **C**. In the dialog box that appears disregard the preset that is selected and make sure that the Preserve Alpha Transparency check box is unselected **D**. Click OK. The result is the same as if you used a Divide Pathfinder filter, with one exception—the overlapped sections have a different color than the remainder of the stripes **E**.

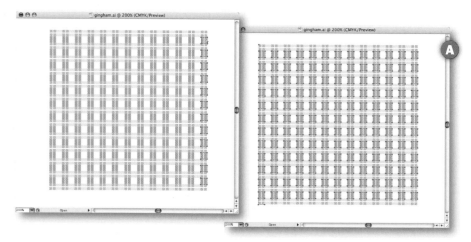

6. Break Out the Colors

The hard part is done! Using the Direct Selection tool select one of the blue stripe segments and press Cmd (Ctrl)-6. Cmd (Ctrl)-6 repeats the last selection option you used. Since you used the Select > Same > Fill Color option earlier, that command is repeated and all the stripe segments with the same color are selected **A**. Change the color of

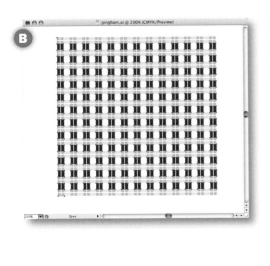

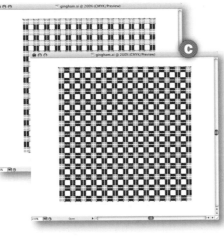

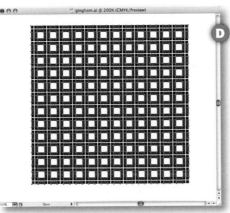

these segments to red and group them (Cmd [Ctrl]-G) **B**. This makes it easier to select them all at once if you want to change the stripe segment color. Select one of the green stripe segments and repeat the same steps (Select > Same > Fill Color) in order to group them **C**. Follow the same steps (Select > Same > Fill Color) with the overlapped segments, but fill these segments with black **D**.

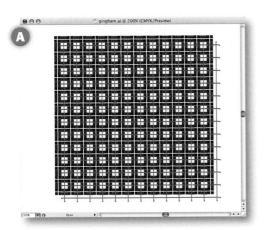

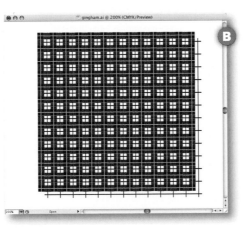

7. Finish the Pattern

Go back to the Preferences dialog box (Cmd [Ctrl]-K) and change the 20 pt Keyboard Increment to **10** pt. Select the white strokes (which should be easy since you grouped them earlier), and Copy (Cmd [Ctrl]-C) and Paste in Back (Cmd [Ctrl]-B). With the arrow key, move the copy down 10 pt and to the right 10 pt. Now make those strokes black **A**.

You're done! If you want to give the pattern even more detail, select the white strokes and give them an opacity of 80% **B**.

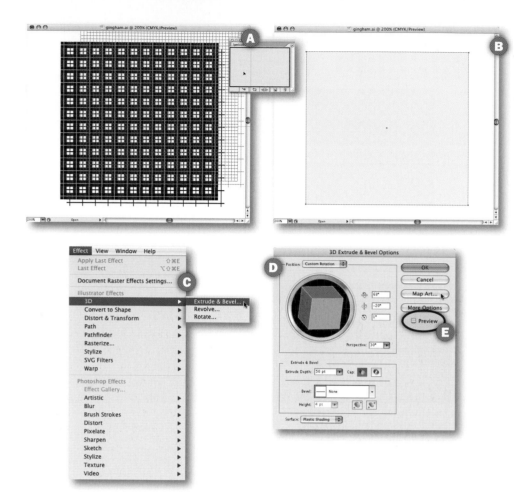

8. Work the Angles

Select the whole pattern and drag it to the Symbols palette to create a new symbol (for more on symbols see "Anatomy of an Infographic" in Chapter 2) **A**. Create a rectangle **B** and then choose Effect > 3D > Extrude & Bevel **C**. In the 3D Extrude & Bevel Options dialog box, rotate the rectangle by dragging the "track cube" to approximate how you want the pattern to "lie" on the ground **D**. Be sure to select the Preview check box so that you can see the relationship to your other artwork **E**. If you like, you can also add a little perspective **F**.

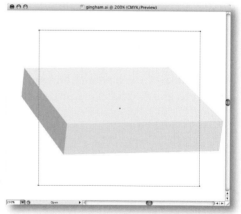

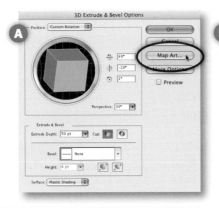

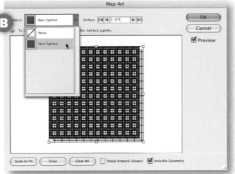

9. Lay the Pattern on the Ground

When you are satisfied with the angle of the rectangle, click the Map Art button **A**. A Map Art dialog box pops up. Select the Symbol drop-down menu and find the symbol of the pattern you made earlier **B**.

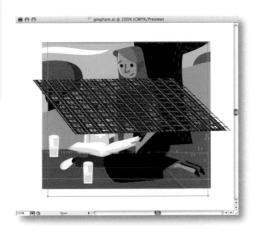

10. Apply the Mapped Artwork

Select the Invisible Geometry check box to make the background rectangle invisible since the rectangle is only acting as a "surface" to lay your pattern on. Be sure to select the Preview check box to see the pattern displayed on the artboard. Click OK to apply the mapped artwork, and then click OK again to apply the Extrude & Bevel options.

11. Mask the Pattern

Finally, paste the rotated pattern into a mask in front of an object filled with a background color. ▥

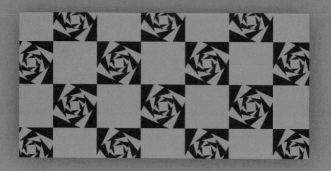

Create a Quilt Pattern

Create an easy pattern by repeating your transformations.

1. Plan Your Design

While there are a lot of patterns that you can find online, why not create your own custom pattern? Sketch out some ideas and then create a new document in Illustrator. If your pattern is geometric and repeating, you can just start with one panel. Then once you have one design completed, you can open a document that is either a 1:1 ratio with your project or some smaller scale version and duplicate the panel as needed to fill the area of your quilt.

2. Create Your First Shape

Let's keep it simple and use just a 5 by 5 inch square as the first element. Use a no fill, black stroke color scheme to start with.

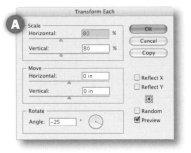
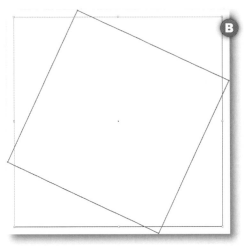

3. Transform and Copy Next Element

For this pattern, you'll need to scale and rotate the next square. To do this, select your element and choose Object > Transform > Transform Each. In the Transform Each dialog box **A**, enter your desired values. Make the square slightly smaller and rotate it to the right about 25 degrees. Make sure the Preview check box is selected so you can view your transformation. Click Copy **B**.

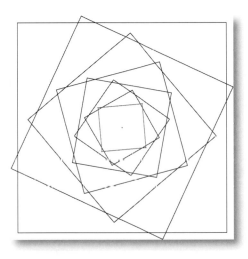

4. Do It Again...and Again

Choose Object > Transform > Transform Again or use the keyboard equivalent Cmd (Ctrl)-D. Repeat this step for as many objects as you want to create.

5. Fill Your Shapes with Color

Select your shapes and fill them with any colors or patterns you desire. For all shapes, set the stroke to None.

6. Trim and Edit as Needed

If you need to trim or edit any shapes, the Pathfinder palette is a great tool to use. Trim the edges of your squares using the Divide button in the Pathfinder palette.

7. Duplicate the Pattern

Create a 35 x 55 inch file for your project and copy and paste your pattern panel into it. Next, create a solid colored 5 inch square and alternate it with your pattern. After doing two rows, simply select both rows and Option (Alt)-drag down to the next row. Press Cmd (Ctrl)-D (Object > Transform > Transform Again) three times, and finish your quilt by Option (Alt)-dragging your final row. ▥

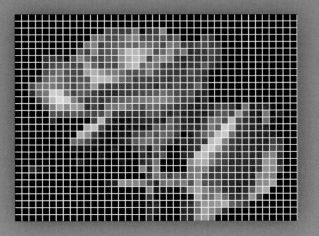

Create a Mosaic for a Tile Project

Start with any raster image and create a mosaic for your next custom tile project.

1. Create a New Document

Create a new document the size of your desired project. For this example, create a 24 x 36 inch file.

2. Place Your Image

You may first want to size the image to fit your project dimensions prior to importing the image into your Illustrator document. Then choose File > Place. Select your file and click Place.

Object Mosaic

Current Size	New Size	
Width: 24 in	Width: 24 in	OK
Height: 36 in	Height: 36 in	Cancel

Tile Spacing	Number of Tiles	
Width: 0.09 in	Width: 22	Use Ratio
Height: 0.09 in	Height: 33	

Options

Constrain Ratio: ⦿ Width ◯ Height

Result: ⦿ Color ◯ Gray

☐ Resize using Percentages
☐ Delete Raster

3. Create the Mosaic

Choose Filter > Create Object Mosaic. In the Object Mosaic dialog box, enter your desired specs (see "Insight: The Object Mosaic Dialog Box") and click OK.

Unfortunately, the dialog box doesn't give you a live preview. That means you might have to tweak your values several times to get the mosaic just right. You'll want enough tiles to capture the details, but not so many that the mosaic turns into an overly complex job.

INSIGHT

The Object Mosaic Dialog Box. Use this dialog box to specify the overal dimensions of your mosaic, as well as the number and proportions of its constituent tiles and the spacing between them.

New Size: The dimensions of your finished mosaic.

Tile Spacing: If your file is the same size as your actual project, you'll want the space between your tiles to be between 1/16 and 1/8 inch. Tile experts recommend a spacing of no larger than 1/8 inch.

Number of Tiles: Here's where a little math comes into play. For this project, let's use 1-inch square tiles (square mosaic tiles commonly come in sizes ranging from 3/8 of an inch to 2 inches). Leaving room for about 1/16 to 1/8 of an inch space between the tiles, using 22 tiles across and 33 tiles down should work. That leaves 2 inches in width and 3 inches in height for the tile spacing. Divide 2 inches by 23 spaces and 3 inches by 35 spaces. That results in .087 inches in width and .086 inches in height for tile spacing. Illustrator rounds both values up to .09.

Use Ratio: Clicking this button gives you square tiles. If you clicked Constrain Ratio: Width, Illustrator adjusts Number of Tiles: Height to give you square tiles and maintain the image's aspect ratio. If you clicked Constrain Ratio: Height, it adjusts Number of Tiles: Width.

Constrain Ratio: Choose whether you want to constrain your ratio to Width or Height.

Result: Choose color or gray tiles.

Resize using Percentages: Enter new sizes as percentages of the old dimensions.

Delete Raster: Delete the raster image after the mosaic is made. We recommend not selecting this option since you probably won't get the mosaic right on the first try. You can always delete the raster image later.

4. Hide Your Raster Image

Your raster image has now been converted into a grid of squares **A**. Select your image and choose Object > Hide > Selection to better view your mosaic **B**. Obviously, if necessary, you can tweak the colors of the individual tiles by selecting each one with your Direct Selection tool.

Not happy with the result? Try the process again with some different settings.

5. Take Another Look

Here is an example of another image **A** used as the basis for a mosaic **B**. You can now take your file and have it printed inexpensively on an oversized printer at a copy service center and use it as a template. Or simply use it as a guide during your tiling project. █

5

DESIGNING
WITH
ILLUSTRATOR

Going Beyond
Shapes and Paths

YOU KNOW HOW IT IS when you live with someone for awhile. You start to take on each other's characteristics and habits. Pretty soon, it seems like you're more alike than different. That appears to be the case with the programs in the Creative Suite. As they've matured, each has adopted many of the same tools and features as its creative cousins. But despite their similarities, each program still has its strengths and primary focus. What the applications were initially created to do is *still* what they do best. In Chapter 7, "Integrating Illustrator and Photoshop," we talk about using Photoshop to complement Illustrator. In this chapter, we take a brief look at using Illustrator and InDesign and what each program brings to the creative table.

Creating 3D Product Labels

Using the real-world experience of Nana Mae's Organics, we show you how you can use Illustrator, along with Photoshop, to quickly and effectively

mock up a series of 3D product labels for bottles. It might sound complicated, but don't worry. We show you each step along the way, so that you can create a similar project should the opportunity arise.

Pluck Artwork from a PDF

If you have ever been under the gun and needed the vector logo of a client immediately, you'll appreciate this tidbit. By opening any PDF in Illustrator, even one with multiple pages, you can pluck artwork from the document and use it as you would any other vector graphic. We also suggest a few other ways to use that PDF once you have it opened in Illustrator.

Time for Text

Besides being one of the most powerful vector drawing programs on the planet,

Illustrator has also become pretty adept at handling type. While its cousin InDesign is the star when it comes to dealing with large quantities of type, Illustrator holds its own, especially when you're using type in expressive and artistic ways. Whole books are dedicated to creating interesting and exciting display type with Illustrator. We have just enough room here to offer a couple of tips that can help you become more productive using type. For example, you can format a piece of text and then use the Eyedropper tool to quickly apply the attributes to other text. And if you've ever wondered why Illustrator offers two drop shadows, wonder no more. Check out the section "Using Drop Shadows" to find out which is best for your particular application. We also show you how to wrap a block of text around either vector or raster images.

InDesign or Illustrator?

InDesign and Illustrator are two powerful programs with a lot of common tools. How do you determine which is best to use for your project?

While it can be argued that whatever works, works, and whichever program you're the most efficient and quickest with may be the best, each program does have its core competencies that it does particularly well.

InDesign—The Pride of Page Layout

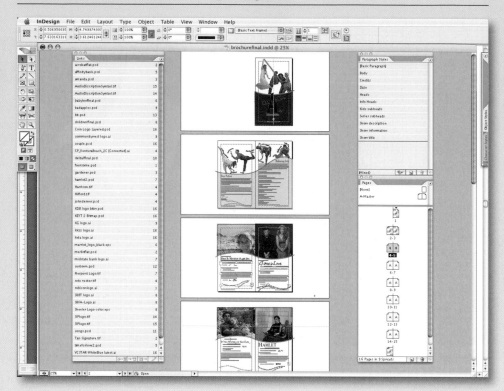

If your project is multipaged, the choice between programs is a no-brainer. Illustrator is still restricted to single page files, whereas InDesign graciously allows for 9999 pages. When it comes to long documents, InDesign has some serious organizing features that allow you to perform functions such as automatically generating a Table of Contents and converting reader spreads to printer spreads (imposition) via the InBooklet command (File > InBooklet). InDesign is also superior when it comes to handling large quantities of text. The tools and features for expert typesetting are part of what InDesign does best. Features such as Story Editor (a built-in word processor), nested styles, the ability to build tables, multiple master pages, data merge (personalizing documents from a database), and XML support enable you to have a fast and productive publishing workflow. On the image side, InDesign is a good program to use if you have large quantities of placed images. InDesign supports asset management via its Library palette, allowing you to store frequently used graphics. In addition, InDesign's preflighting and packaging features let you run a prepress check of your file and then collect all of your fonts and links necessary for hand off to your print vendor.

Illustrator—The Ruler of All Artwork Drawn

Got a complex drawing? Hands down, Illustrator is the program *du jour*. While InDesign now has quite a few of Illustrator's tools, such as the Pen tool, and the ability to handle transparency, drop shadows, gradients, and type on a path, it still doesn't hold a candle to Illustrator's superior drawing capabilities. Features such as masking, enveloping, tracing artwork, nondestructive effects, sublayer support,

and creating 3D objects all fall into Illustrator's domain. And while InDesign does enable you to repurpose layouts for use on the Web with its Package for GoLive command, Illustrator's Web-friendly tools, from creating symbols to the Save for Web command to the ability to export directly to Flash, make it the program of choice for creating and preparing artwork for the Web.

But let's say you have a single-page project with equal amounts of text and artwork. You don't need sophisticated type handling, and the drawings are pretty basic. Then the decision comes down to the little nuances of each program that are way too numerous to mention here. And, of course, the program you feel most comfortable and productive working in will probably play a major role in your decision…as it should.

Mocking Up 3D Product Labels

Use a combination of Photoshop, the 3D Revolve effect, and symbols to mock up a product.

Nana Mae Bottle.ai @ 100% (R...

100%

1. Place the Photoshop File

A series of product shots for the Nana Mae Organic Web site needs to be produced quickly. However, the only product photograph available is of a single bottle. But the label is fuzzy and off-color, the edges are frayed, and the bottle is not lit correctly **A**. Fortunately, the lighting and background can be corrected in Photoshop **B** and original vector label artwork can be applied to the bottle by using the 3D Revolve effect in Illustrator.

Place the Photoshop file of the bottle as a template layer into the same Illustrator file as the label artwork **C**.

2. Create a Simplified Template of the Label

Since the label artwork is so complex, involving text, multiple rules, photographs, and placed graphics **A**, mapping the label artwork to start with would slow the application to a crawl and the Progress dialog box would pop up constantly **B**. To avoid this, create a copy of the label artwork (you'll need the original for the final artwork at the end). Working on the copy of the label artwork, break down the artwork into its essential elements, but keep the artwork area dimensions exactly the same **C**. This label template will be used as a temporary placeholder for the real label artwork.

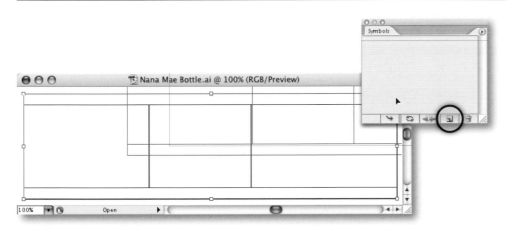

3. Make a Symbol of the Template

Select the label template artwork and create a symbol of it by dragging the artwork into the Symbols palette or by clicking the New Symbol button at the bottom of the palette.

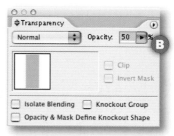

4. Create a 3D Cylinder

Using the photograph template of the bottle as a guide, create a rectangle with a color fill and a stroke of None that is half the width of the bottle **A**. Since the 3D Revolve effect rotates artwork from the left axis, position the rectangle on the right half of the bottle so that when it revolves the cylinder will appear directly on top of the bottle. Give the rectangle an opacity of 50% in the Transparency palette to view the photograph of the bottle underneath **B**.

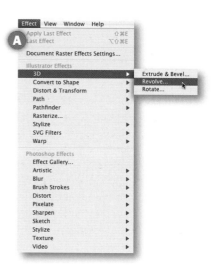

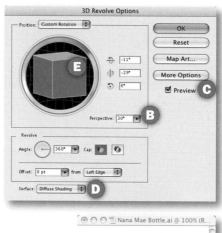

5. Revolve the Rectangle

Select the rectangle and create a cylinder by choosing Effect > 3D > Revolve **A**. In the 3D Revolve Options dialog box, give the cylinder a slight 30° perspective **B**, select Preview **C** to see how the cylinder is positioned with the photograph of the bottle, and choose Surface: Diffuse Shading **D**. Then by rotating the track cube **E**, carefully line up the curvature of the 3D cylinder as closely to the photograph as possible **F**.

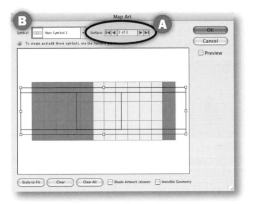

6. Map the Label Template

While you're still in the 3D Revolve Options dialog box, click the Map Art button to bring up the Map Art dialog box. Next, click through the different surface views until you get the side surface **A**. Then on the Symbol menu in the dialog box **B**, select the label template.

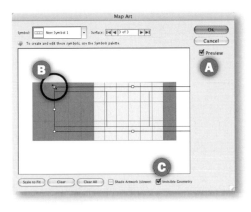

7. Position the Label Template

In the Map Art dialog box, select Preview **A** to see how the label template is positioned with the bottle. In the preview area, the shaded areas indicate surface areas that are hidden from view in the current rotation setting. The next part is a little tricky. Proportionally resize the template symbol to fit the bottle by clicking one of the corner handles and holding down the Shift key (see "Caution: The Finicky Scaling Function") **B**. Once the template is resized and positioned to overlap the photograph of the bottle, select Invisible Geometry **C** to hide the cylinder from view **D**. Then click OK twice to close both dialog boxes and return to the artboard.

CAUTION

The Finicky Scaling Function. The sizing function in the Map Art dialog is super sensitive when it comes to scaling proportionally using the Shift key. When you finish dragging with the mouse to scale, be sure to release the Shift key *after* letting go of the mouse button or else the template symbol won't scale properly. Unfortunately, there is no undo function in the Map Art dialog box, so you only get one shot at it. Make a mistake, and you'll have to Clear and start over again.

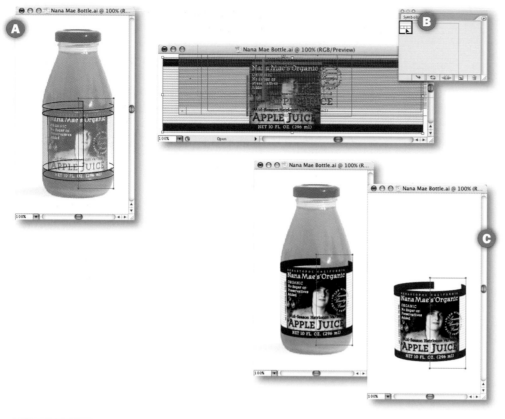

8. Swap the Symbol

Now that the curvature of the template symbol matches up to the photograph of the bottle, select the 3D object you just created and set the opacity back to 100% in the Transparency palette **A**. Then select the original, complex label artwork, and while holding down the Option (Alt) key, drag the artwork on top of the thumbnail of the template in the Symbols palette **B**. By swapping the template artwork with the original, complex artwork, all instances of the symbol are also changed, including the symbol that was mapped to the cylinder **C**.

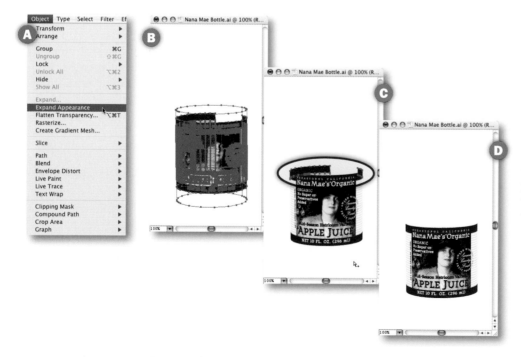

9. Expand the Cylinder and Clean Up the Label

Since we need to create additional labels for this bottle, duplicate the layer, hide the original, select the 3D cylinder/rectangle on the duplicated layer, and choose Object > Expand Appearance **A** to break down the mapped label symbol into editable paths **B**. After the artwork is expanded, select the extraneous paths (the section of the label that was wrapped around to the opposite side of the cylinder) **C** and delete them **D**.

10. Composite the New Label in Photoshop

Now hide all the artwork on the artboard except for the mapped label and save the file. In Photoshop, open the Illustrator file (making sure the resolution is the same as the bottle photograph file), and then copy and paste the new label artwork into the bottle photograph file. Move the label into position, add a slight gradient shadow to the label to match the lighting of the bottle, and you're done **A**! The result is a crisp, clean label that replaces the fuzzy, frayed one underneath.

Creating additional labels is easily done by going back to the Illustrator artwork and swapping the label symbol with different versions of label artwork (which have the same dimensions) **B**. ▥

Extracting Artwork from a PDF and More

Take advantage of Illustrator's native file format to comp, edit, or copy a PDF document.

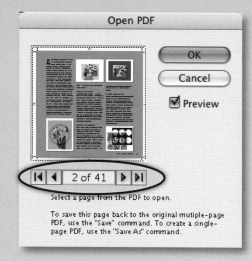

Opening a PDF File in Illustrator

Illustrator is extremely PDF friendly. In fact, it can open just about any flavor of PDF (Illustrator, Photoshop, InDesign, Acrobat, and virtually any other program). Note that when opening generic PDF files (those created outside of Illustrator), certain elements may not be converted or imported exactly the way they appeared in the original file. In addition, if you do not have the same font that was used in the original document loaded on your system, you will experience font substitution, which will also alter the appearance of the PDF. But other than that, there are numerous opportunities that can be garnered from opening a PDF file in Illustrator.

To open a PDF file in Illustrator, even one consisting of multiple pages, choose File > Open and select the PDF file. In the Open PDF dialog box, select a page from the PDF to open. You can navigate through the pages by using the forward or backward arrows. When you have located your desired page, click OK.

After opening the PDF file, you can perform several useful tasks:

- **Comp an illustration:** Do you need to get the exact size of the area where your illustration will be placed in the layout? If your client has provided you with a PDF layout, it's as simple as opening the page your artwork will appear on and copying and pasting the placeholder window into your artwork file.

- **Pick up colors:** If your PDF was converted to native Illustrator objects, you can match the color of a layout by opening the PDF file and using the Eyedropper tool to sample a color. If, however, your PDF didn't convert the page elements to native Illustrator objects, the color you sample will just be an RGB screen representation of that color and not the actual color value from the original PDF.

- **Modify a single page:** Do you need to modify a single page in a multipage document but don't have the original file it was created with? Use Illustrator to open a single page in the PDF file, modify the page, and then save the file. The PDF file will still open as a multipage document in any PDF reader and will include the changes you made to that single page.

- **Grab a logo:** If you're on a deadline and can't get the artwork for a logo from your client in time, try downloading a PDF file from the company's Web site. Open the file in Illustrator and use the Selection tool to select and copy the logo into a new file. Most likely, the logo was placed in the PDF document as an EPS file, which is, of course, readable and editable (for example, to scale without degradation) in Illustrator.

Using the Eyedropper with Text

One of the more underutilized features of the Eyedropper tool is its ability to sample and apply text attributes including font character, size, color, and so on without selecting the type objects.

Position and Fill the Eyedropper

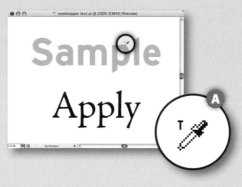

Select the Eyedropper tool and position the eyedropper over an unselected type object. When you hover close enough to a type object to take a sample of the attributes, a small "T" will appear to the left of the eyedropper **A**. Click with the Eyedropper tool and the icon will change and look like it has been "filled" **B**.

Apply the Type Attribute

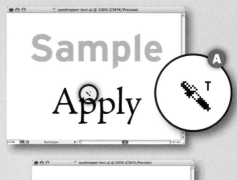

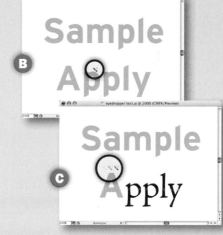

Hold down the Option (Alt) key and the Eyedropper tool will change orientation and go from angling down from the right (the sample mode) to angling down from the left (the apply mode) **A**. Now with the Option (Alt) key held down, position the Eyedropper tool over another unselected type object (the small "T" will appear again when you have the type targeted) and click the mouse. The type object will take on the attributes of the sampled type **B**.

One alternative to clicking and changing the whole type object is to click and drag over a section of the type object to change only parts of the type object **C**. 🕮

Using Drop Shadows

Knowing the difference between Illustrator's two drop shadows—one is a filter and the other is an effect—can determine whether you use one or the other.

If you've poked around Illustrator a bit, you no doubt have stumbled upon the drop shadow feature. And maybe you stumbled upon it again under a different menu heading. What's up with that? Well, although their results may look the same, they are in fact different in many ways.

Filter drop shadow:

drop shadow

Effect drop shadow:

drop shadow

Filter Drop Shadow

Create Separate Shadows checked

Create Separate Shadows unchecked

Filters are destructive. By destructive we don't mean they will harm your artwork. We mean that they will change the underlying structure of the object. With raster images, this means pixels are altered. With vector images, this means paths are altered. In addition, once the filter is applied, you cannot go back and edit or remove the filter. The Drop Shadow filter is a bit unique in that it does not alter any paths. But it does share the characteristic that once a shadow is applied, it can't be edited or removed.

If you haven't checked out the Drop Shadow filter, here's the lowdown. With the Selection tool, select your object or type and choose Filter > Stylize > Drop Shadow. The Drop Shadow dialog box appears **A** where you can specify options such as Blend Mode, Opacity, Offset (how close the shadow is to the object), Blur (the softness of the shadow), Color, and Darkness amounts. Be sure to select Preview and tweak these options to get your desired shadow effect. Note that you will find the Create Separate Shadow option only on the Filter menu. This option places a separate shadow behind each object. If the option isn't selected, the shadows are all placed together behind the bottommost object **B**.

Effect Drop Shadow

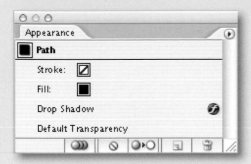

INSIGHT

Raster Settings. When applying raster filters or effects such as drop shadows, glows, and feathers, you need to be aware that the Document Raster Effects Settings (on the Effect menu) impact the result of the filter or effect. Illustrator uses these raster settings to determine the resolution for the rasterization of the filter or effect. When working with Web graphics, use a screen resolution, and when working with graphics intended to be offset printed, stick with a minimum of High.

Effects are always nondestructive, meaning that they do not alter the underlying structure of an object. Imagine yourself wearing a costume: You may look like Darth Vader, but underneath the costume it's still you. You can alter the costume and take it off. You can do so with effects as well. Effects are also "live," so you can edit them to your heart's content. If you've lost your love for a particular effect, that's no problem. Simply eliminate the effect by deleting it from the Appearance palette. Once you apply an effect, in this case by choosing Effect > Stylize > Drop Shadow, Illustrator adds the effect as an attribute in the Appearance palette. Once in the Appearance palette, simply double-click the effect to edit it. For more on the Appearance palette, see Chapter 2, "Freeform Drawing and Geometric Shapes."

Another big advantage to using effects over filters is that if you alter your shape, the filter drop shadow will not dynamically update to the edited shape. However, if the drop shadow is an effect, it will update to match the altered shape. The only downside is that effects are slightly more memory intensive, meaning that they may take a little longer to apply and use a little more space to save, but that's it.

Oborem vent utpat. Duisit ad mod do duisl iusto con henibh erostrud elismol orperos eu facilla augiam nullum ilit ute voloborem nismodit ulla ad te magnim vent ip ea cor sim dolendreet ate dolesed euipit erilit ullandrem ametue veriusc illaor alit venim in henibh enibh ex enis nos nos et, quissequip exeros augiat prat.

Raessendipis dolor alis nulpute modolortie magna adigna facin henis   duis nostrud tatissequis nullan vel dolestrud min etuerilit endre digna feu faccummodio cor sit lamet lummy nulla facilit et, sequat vullutat amonsequam veliqui smodolore conullandrem veliquat pratuer iril et laorper in ut adipis digniatie faccum quam quisi.

Ud eu facil ea feuis at wissequisci euis nisi blandiam iriusci duisit luptat. Ut lorper il er adit prat, si blam dolessendit loreet, summole ndignisl ullamco mmodolorem dip ent nostrud tatio conum et adigna feuguerci blaoreet am, veraesed tem dolum dolorperos eugait pratum vel il ullandiam venim ate dionsed tie tinciduisi.

Elisis nibh et, conulla at velissisi.

Luptat. Alit pratumsandit vullut alismolent alit prat alit ulla feugait wismod tie magna ad dolore min henibh euguer in ea ad delis dolorercilit dolore corem nostismod enit il esequat.

Nit, seniatu erostrud tat.

Sequis eugue dionsenis augue commolo rperat, quisit amet velis auguerc illuptat utate tate dit, sed del dolore deleniscipit luptatio euiscilit, sequi exeraesed digniat inisseniat deliquat. Ut nullum erosting elit lut in hent ad do

ILLUSTRATION BY ZACH TRENHOLM

Wrap Type Around a Shape

Take advantage of shapes to breathe life into your type.

Ex elismod olummolorem vullaor susto dolortisi ex eu feu faci exerciduipis eugiat. Qui euguit, sit la conullut volorti scincil eugiatuer sis nim nos nit augiatem ea commodit laortie velestrud doloreet laorper ostrud elessequis exer suscil ipit aut iustrud do dolorper incidui tat, corper ad dolobor sumsan eumsan veliquate vel ullam iniscil iquam, quamet, core consequ ismodolorper incidunt wis alit ulla corem do consed tatem delendigna am, quipisis nullam ipis alisl ut luptat. Ut ver sequat. Ed min et prat ut in et adiamet vel do odolor aciliquisl illandio conum vulluptatkfjkj hkd.

Oborem vent utpat. Duisit ad mod do duisl iusto con henibh erostrud elismol orperos eu facilla augiam nullum ilit ute voloborem nismodit ulla ad te magnim vent ip ea cor sim dolendreet ate dolesed euipit erilit ullandrem ametue veriusc illaor alit venim in henibh enibh ex enis nos nos et, quissequip exeros augiat prat.

Raessendipis dolor alis nulpute modolortie magna adigna facin henis duis nostrud tatissequis nullan vel dolestrud min etuerilit endre digna feu faccummodio cor sit lamet lummy nulla facilit et, sequat vullutat amonsequam veliqui smodolore conullandrem veliquat pratuer iril et laorper in ut adipis digniatie faccum quam quisi.

Ud eu facil ea feuis at wissequisci euis nisi blandiam iriusci duisit luptat. Ut lorper il er adit prat, si blam dolessendit loreet, summole ndignisl ullamco mmodolorem dip ent nostrud tatio conum et adigna feuguerci blaoreet am, veraesed tem dolum dolorperos eugait pratum vel il ullandiam venim ate dionsed tie tinciduisi.

Elisis nibh et, conulla at velissisi.

Luptat. Alit pratumsandit vullut alismolent alit prat alit ulla feugait wismod tie magna ad dolore min henibh euguer in ea ad delis dolorercilit irit dolore corem nostismod enit il esequat.

Nit, seniatu erostrud tat.

Sequis eugue dionsenis augue commolo rperat, quisit amet velis auguerc illuptat utate tate dit, sed del dolore deleniscipit luptatio euiscilit, sequi exeraesed digniat inisseniat deliquat. Ut nullum erosting elit lut in hent ad do odit wis dolobore con henim adiate ver autpat iusciliqui tem vel utem wenis del dolor augue eumsandre magnism odiamco nummole sectet la alit eum alit veriurero od magnim nonsequ ismodit digniamet prat am nullut incincip ex et wis nisi' dolorem adiamco nulputpat, qui et, volore corem zzrit non utpat dolorting eugiat verciliqu. doloborperit ad molor sum zzril ut augue cortionse magnisi ea facipis senibh ex exero con utet,

1. Create Your Type

Using the Type tool, create your desired type. Be sure to create area type rather than point type. To do so, drag a rectangle with the Type tool to define your bounding area. Then type so that your text is contained within the boundary of the space you defined.

INSIGHT

Wrapping Text. Illustrator enables you to wrap text around just about everything—type, objects, or images. If you import an image with transparency, Illustrator will recognize that transparency and only wrap around the opaque pixels.

2. Create Your Wrap Object

Create your Illustrator object(s) or import an image. For details on importing Photoshop files, see Chapter 7. The wrap object must be above your type in order for the wrap to work. Therefore, if by chance you created your type after your objects were drawn or your image was imported, select your object or image and choose Object > Arrange > Bring to Front. If you are using layers, you can also arrange your stacking order via the Layers palette.

3. Make the Text Wrap

Select the artwork and choose Object > Text Wrap > Make Text Wrap. You might get an alert that tells you the text will wrap around all objects in the current selection. Click OK.

4. Fine-tune the Wrap

With the text and the wrap object still selected, choose Object > Text Wrap > Text Wrap Options. In the dialog box, specify your offset amount. This setting adjusts the amount of space between your type and the wrap object. Increase the value to move the type farther away from the object. Select the Invert Wrap option to wrap your text around the opposite side of the object. To undo the text wrap, choose Object > Text Wrap > Release Text Wrap. ▥

6

ILLUSTRATOR AND THE WEB

Integrating Illustrator into Your Online Workflow

SET UP FOR THE WEB *164*

EXPORT WITH SAVE FOR WEB *166*

PIXELS, POINTS, AND STROKES *168*

SLICING IN ILLUSTRATOR *171*

CREATE FLEXIBLE HEADLINES *175*

CREATE A WEB LAYOUT *181*

EXPORTING TO FLASH *186*

FLASH EXPORT OPTIONS *194*

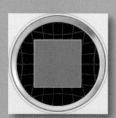

CREATE A SIMPLE FLASH ANIMATION *196*

AS ILLUSTRATORS AND designers, we know that it's a constant challenge trying to get our prints to come within a reasonable proximity of what we see on our screen. But what about just being able to get what we want onscreen to look good, well, onscreen? Sounds like a no-brainer, but in actuality it can be tricky and sometimes downright baffling. This chapter helps you get started on the right track, guides you along the way, and assists you in getting your creation up on the Web to be admired by all.

Setting Up and Saving Out

Correctly setting up your file is a critical component in getting the color you want displayed on the Web. From choosing the correct color space to the right ICC profile, we'll show you what you need to know to create eye-catching artwork for the Web. We'll also explain the importance of thinking in pixels, mea-

suring in points when you have to, and using whole numbers. And to make sure your final product is ideal for the Web, we'll dissect the Save for Web feature, which enables you to preview how your optimized artwork will appear online.

Slicing and Dicing

Okay, maybe we won't discuss dicing, but we'll definitely describe slicing. Compared to Photoshop or ImageReady, Illustrator has more than its share of peculiarities when it comes to slicing. We'll explain how to work around those quirks and make a smooth transition from the vector world of Illustrator to the raster environment of the Web.

Making Headlines

Creating great-looking type on the Web can be a headache. We'll show you how Illustrator actually has advantages over its raster-based cousins—Photoshop and ImageReady—when it comes to

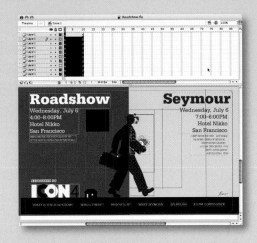

creating type for the screen. In addition, we'll show you how to change the color of your type and have it automatically update in your Web design program.

Creating a Web Layout and Exporting to Flash

Is CSS a mysterious acronym to you? Not to worry. In the last section, we'll provide the nitty-gritty details of creating a CSS-based Web layout. We'll also share the fine points of exporting to Flash and what to do in instances when Illustrator and Flash don't play together nicely, such as when using text, clipping masks, and placed images. We end the chapter with a fun and simple project on creating a frame-by-frame animation using Illustrator and Flash.

INSIGHT

What Is CSS? Cascading Style Sheets (CSS) is a stylesheet language used to define colors, fonts, layout, and the other visual characteristics of a typical Web page. Although much too complex to go into any amount of detail in this book, it is the *de facto* standard for creating a Web page.

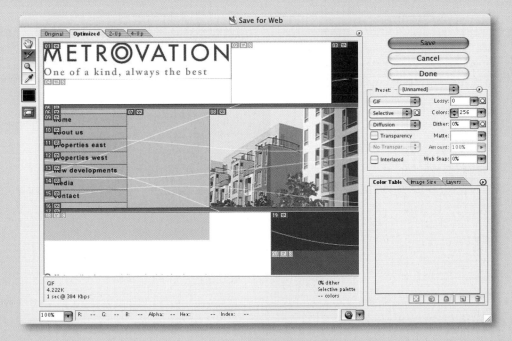

Set Up for the Web

When you start an Illustrator project that you intend to use for a Web site or other nonprint destination, be sure to perform the following tasks before you begin.

Set the Correct Color Space

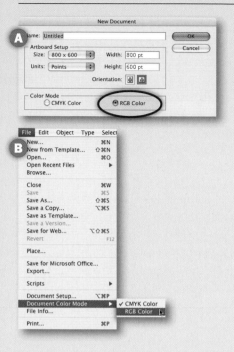

In the New Document dialog box, select RGB Color as your file's color mode **A**. Of course, you can change the color mode at any time by choosing File > Document Color Mode > RGB Color **B**. However, since the gamut of colors in the RGB color space is much larger than the CMYK color space, by starting off in RGB you'll have a much wider range of colors to choose from. Also, remember that all Web authoring programs (including Flash) are based on RGB—specifically, hexadecimal values (e.g., #E3E3B4).

Set the Color Profile

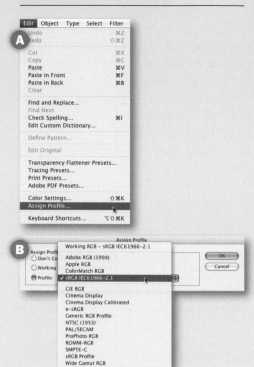

Although there is no way to target your color with any degree of accuracy to the billions of PCs and Macs browsing the Internet, you can at least try to set your profile to the color space that the majority of users have, which is sRGB IEC61966-2.1 (a name only a software programmer could love). To set your color profile, choose Edit > Assign Profile **A**. In the Assign Profile dialog box, select Profile and choose sRGB IEC61966-2.1 from the menu **B**.

Check the Proof Setup Setting

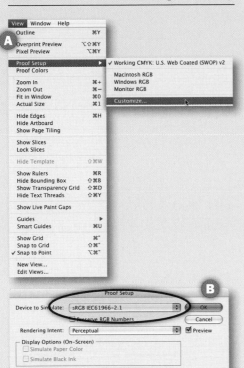

For RGB work, Proof Setup is probably the most important setting of all. You need to make sure that you are previewing your artwork or design based on the intended target monitor. Many times the default will be CMYK, even though you have chosen RGB as your color mode. To choose your Proof Setup setting choose View > Proof Setup > Customize **A**. In the Proof Setup dialog box that appears, choose sRGB IEC61966-2.1 from the Device to Simulate pop-up menu **B**.

Pixel Preview

Enabling the Pixel Preview option lets you view your artwork or design in a simulated 72 dpi raster-based setting (as opposed to Illustrator's native PostScript-based, resolution independent view). This option is very useful for determining details such as the readability of a font at small sizes and how line weights and edges appear in a rasterized setting (see "Pixels, Points, and Strokes" later in this chapter for more about pixels and line weights). To enable the Pixel Preview option choose View > Pixel Preview.

Snap to Pixel

With Pixel Preview enabled, the Snap to Pixel option also becomes available to you and is turned on by default. Snap to Pixel ensures that any object created or moved will "snap" to the nearest pixel. Remember, Snap to *Pixel* refers to snapping to a unit of measure as opposed to Snap to *Point,* which refers to snapping to a "point" of a path. ▥

INSIGHT

Pixels vs. Points. Points (a unit of measure) and pixels are basically the same unit; however, points can be divided into smaller units (.5, .25), whereas pixels cannot.

Export with Save for Web

The Save for Web dialog box shares a common interface with its counterpart in Photoshop. Both function as a stripped-down version of the Adobe raster-based Web application ImageReady and contain many of its primary features. To access the Save for Web dialog box either choose File > Save for Web or press Cmd-Option (Ctrl-Alt)-Shift-S. This dialog box has a ton of features—too many to explain here. We'll give you an overview of the important features and recommend that you read *How to Wow: Photoshop CS2 for the Web* (Peachpit, 2006), our sister book in this series, for more detailed information.

Anatomy of the Save for Web Dialog Box

A *Tabs:* Across the top are four different view tabs: Original shows how the artwork appears in its original Illustrator context; Optimized shows the rasterized view of the artwork based on the optimization settings; 2-Up shows both the original and optimized views; and 4-Up shows the original and three optimized views of your choice.

B *File type and size:* File type, size, simulated download times, and settings are displayed based on the settings you select.

C *Color values:* You can view color values by placing your cursor over the artwork in the preview area, and the color information under the cursor will display here.

D *Preview menu:* The name is slightly deceptive because aside from an item that lets you preview your graphic as it would look if its colors were dithered in a browser, the rest of the menu lets you choose the connection speed the simulated download times are based on.

E *Preset menu:* Although you can choose a preset setting from the pop-up menu **F**, this panel is where you can select numerous optimization settings and is not limited to the presets. In the Optimized File Format menu **G**, you can choose different file formats including GIF, JPEG, PNG-8, PNG-24, and WBMP. And because Illustrator is a vector-based application, there are two additional options not found in Photoshop—SWF and SVG.

H *Optimize menu:* Actually, this is more like an optimize *options* menu. In this menu are various settings that relate to preset settings, file size, slices, and output settings.

I *Color Table:* This table displays the colors present in your document when saved in the GIF, PNG, and WBMP file formats.

J *Image Size:* This is a very handy panel for reducing or enlarging your exported files without modifying your original artwork (and since PostScript is not a raster-based file format, enlarge to your heart's content). Remember to click Apply to set the modified dimensions. Also, since the size modifications don't affect the original artwork, it's a good idea to write down the percentage that you are sizing the artwork to in case you need to size other artwork to the same ratio.

K *Layers:* If you choose to export the layers of your file as CSS layers along with the resulting HTML file, here is the place to do it. However, if you are proficient with CSS programming, this isn't the best way to create layers, and if you aren't familiar with CSS, we don't recommend using this option.

L *Tools:* Along the left side of the dialog box you'll find a few basic tools (any of which can be accessed with the same shortcut keys as the main Illustrator program): **M** the Hand tool lets you scroll around the preview area; **N** the Slice Select tool enables you to select single or multiple slices (if you hold down the Shift key); **O** the Zoom tool lets you zoom in or out of the view in your preview window; **P** the Eyedropper tool picks up the color in the preview window and displays it in the small swatch below it **Q**; and **R** the Toggle Slices Visibility button hides or shows your slices. ▦

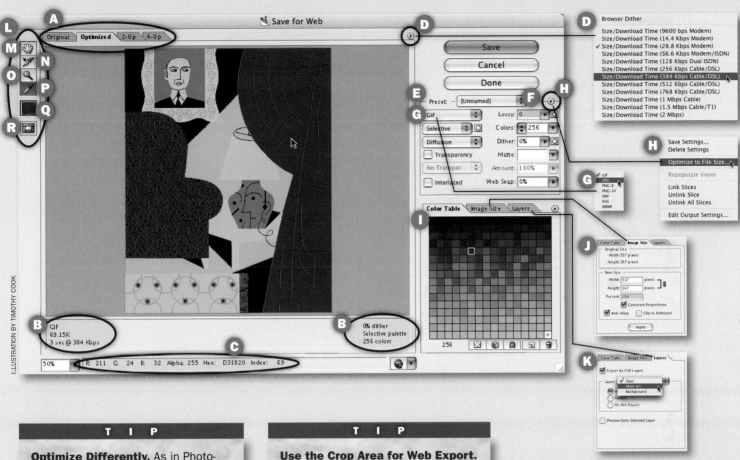

ILLUSTRATION BY TIMOTHY COOK

Save for Web

Original Optimized 2-Up 4-Up

Browser Dither

Size/Download Time (9600 bps Modem)
Size/Download Time (14.4 Kbps Modem)
✓ Size/Download Time (28.8 Kbps Modem)
Size/Download Time (56.6 Kbps Modem/ISDN)
Size/Download Time (128 Kbps Dual ISDN)
Size/Download Time (256 Kbps Cable/DSL)
Size/Download Time (384 Kbps Cable/DSL)
Size/Download Time (512 Kbps Cable/DSL)
Size/Download Time (768 Kbps Cable/DSL)
Size/Download Time (1 Mbps Cable)
Size/Download Time (1.5 Mbps Cable/T1)
Size/Download Time (2 Mbps)

Save
Cancel
Done

Preset: – [Unnamed]

Save Settings...
Delete Settings

Optimize to File Size...

Repopulate Views

Link Slices
Unlink Slice
Unlink All Slices

Edit Output Settings...

GIF   Lossy: 0
Selective   Colors: 256
Diffusion   Dither: 0%
Transparency Matte:
No Transpar... Amount: 100%
Interlaced   Web Snap: 0%

GIF
JPEG
PNG-8
PNG-24
SWF
SVG
WBMP

Color Table   Image Size   Layers

Color Table   Image Size   Layers
Original Size
Width:537 pixels
Height:367 pixels

New Size
Width: 537   pixels
Height: 367 pixels
Percent: 100
Constrain Proportions
Anti-Alias   Clip to Artboard

Apply

GIF
69.15K
3 sec @ 384 Kbps

0% dither
Selective palette
256 colors

256

50%   R: 211 G: 24 B: 32 Alpha: 255 Hex: D31820 Index: 69

Color Table   Image Size   Layers
Export As CSS Layers

Layer   Text
        Main Art
        Background

Preview Only Selected Layer

TIP

Optimize Differently. As in Photoshop, you can individually select slices in the preview window and assign them different export settings in the Optimization Settings panel. For instance, a flat area of color can have a 2-color GIF setting, whereas an adjoining area can have a 256-color GIF setting or be exported as a JPEG.

TIP

Use the Crop Area for Web Export. If you want to export just a part of a file for the Web, draw a rectangle around the desired area, and then make a crop area (see the section "Set Up Your File" in Chapter 1, "Program Foundations"). By creating a crop area, when you use the Save for Web export dialog box, only the art within the crop area will be exported. Using a crop area can also come in handy when you want to create a white border or extra area around your Web graphic.

Pixels, Points, and Strokes

Since Illustrator is a vector-based application (unlike Photoshop and ImageReady, which are raster-based), its files don't make the transition to the raster-based world of the Internet without a little kicking and screaming. Here are a few tips to make the raster jump a little easier.

Think in Pixels

It's important to enable Pixel Preview and Snap to Pixel when creating slices (for more on slices see "Slicing in Illustrator" later in this chapter) and filled rectangle areas of color since they should be measured in whole pixels.

For example, these two rectangles display perfectly with Pixel Preview turned off **A**. But with Pixel Preview turned on you can see the anti-aliasing along the edges **B**. This was due to Snap to Pixel not being turned on when the object was created.

Although the object's measurements displayed in the Transform palette as whole pixels, when the unit of measurement was changed to points, the measurements ended with .5 pt—not whole numbers. In order to display a pixel measurement, Illustrator rounded up the displayed measurement to a whole pixel (remember there is no such thing as a half pixel) and tried to "average" the pixel's color value over two pixels.

Creating slices based on objects with *non*-whole numbered measurements or coordinates can cause the slices to "jump" to the nearest whole pixel, averaging what is displayed to get to that whole pixel **C**. With Pixel Preview and Snap to Pixel turned on, any object drawn will automatically be "snapped" to a whole pixel. With the *x, y* coordinates set to a whole pixel, you can see that the slices are now correctly abutting each other **D**.

When to Measure in Points

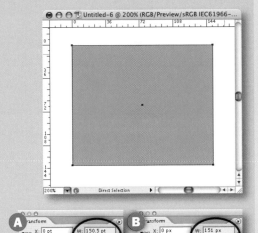

It's preferable to start your document with pixels as your unit of measurement and remain in pixels throughout the creation of your artwork. However, if your document was initially created in CMYK color mode or contains objects created with points as your unit of measurement, then keep your unit of measure as points. For example, an object is drawn with a 150.5 pt width **A**, but if you change the unit of measure to pixels, that width would display as 151 px **B** due to rounding up. By keeping points as the unit of measure, it is easier to catch your mistakes and keep the measurements and positioning of your artwork in whole numbers.

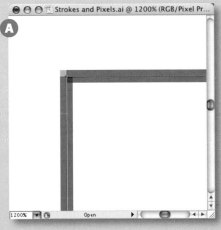

Strokes, Pixels, and Points

Stroked objects bring a different set of problems: By default, a path's stroke is drawn on the center line of the path, so half the stroke weight appears on either side of the path. For instance, the width of a 1 pixel stroke falls 1/2 pixel on either side of the actual path. Consequently, your stroke will display with an anti-aliased edge because the 1 pixel stroke will be averaged over two whole pixels since there is no such thing as a half pixel **A**.

By following these steps you'll be able to solve the problem so the stroke's appearance is nice and crisp:

1. Turn on Preview Bounds: By default, Illustrator uses the vector path to calculate the measurements that are displayed, or when aligning objects. When you turn on Preview Bounds **B**, Illustrator uses the *visual appearance*, not the path, to calculate the measurements.

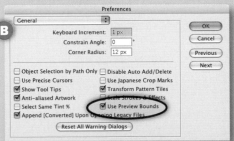

For instance, with Preview Bounds turned *off*, a 10 px x 10 px rectangle with a 2 px stroke attribute will display the value in the Transform palette as 10 px in height and 10 px in width. However, with Preview Bounds turned *on*, that same box will display the value as 12 px in height and 12 px in width. This is because Illustrator is now calculating the width and height of the object's path and adding 1 pixel to all sides for the stroke (since strokes are set to the center of the path, half the stroke falls on either side).

Since it is important to keep all your objects' measurements on a whole pixel or number, you need to start with an accurate number based on the path *and* the stroke. For more information, see "Insight: Preview Bounds, Strokes, and Measurements" on the next page.

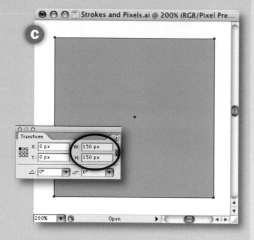

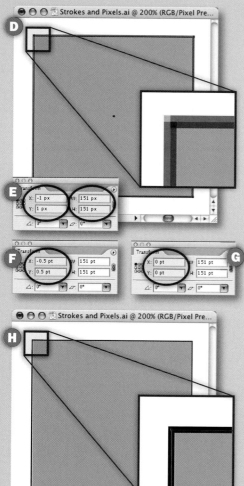

2. Create a rectangle: Enable Pixel Preview. Create a 150 px x 150 px rectangle with a color fill and no stroke. Make sure the rectangle's coordinates are on a whole pixel or number (with Pixel Preview enabled, the Snap to Pixel feature is turned on by default, so the rectangle object's coordinates should automatically be placed on a whole pixel or number) **C**.

3. Add a stroke: Add a 1 pixel stroke to the object, and you'll see that the stroke you created is now anti-aliased **D**. In the Transform palette, the rectangle's x and y coordinates have changed, and 1 pixel has been added to each value **E**.

4. Switch from pixels to points: Change the unit of measurement to points. The value shown in the Transform palette reflects the 1 px stroke falling on either side of the path, or .5 pt. (Remember, since there is no such thing as a half pixel, the pixel measurement displayed was rounded up; thus, viewing the measurement in points is necessary.) By adding a 1 pixel stroke, the area Illustrator uses for measuring the rectangle takes into account the width of the stroke, changing the x and y coordinates by a .5 pt and increasing the total width and height by 1 pt or px to 151 **F**.

5. Fix the coordinates: To correct this problem, change the x and y coordinates back to whole numbers **G**. The stroked box now displays with clean, crisp edges **H**. 🖤

INSIGHT

Align Stroke. In the Stroke palette is an Align Stroke option that positions your stroke on the inside, center, or outside of the path. Theoretically, this should solve the problem of the stroke anti-aliasing since the stroke no longer is drawn halfway on either side of the path. If only life always worked the way it should—unfortunately, due to a display bug, even with Align Stroke enabled the problem still persists.

INSIGHT

Preview Bounds, Strokes, and Measurements. If the Preview Bounds setting is turned off, Illustrator calculates the *x* and *y* coordinates from the actual path, not the stroke. As a result, after adding a 1 pixel stroke, the *x* and *y* coordinates wouldn't change, but the stroke would still be anti-aliased. To correct the appearance, you would need to add .5 to both *x* and *y* values to get the object back "on pixel." When you're trying to keep everything to whole numbers, this is confusing to say the least. It's much easier and less confusing to just turn on Preview Bounds.

CAUTION

Getting Rid of the Stroke. If you change the *x* and *y* coordinates to fix the appearance of a stroke and then decide to get rid of the stroke, remember to change the value of the coordinates back to whole numbers.

Slicing in Illustrator

Slicing refers to cutting up a piece of artwork (in this case Illustrator artwork) for use on a Web page. Slicing in Illustrator is nothing like slicing in Photoshop or ImageReady. Although the tool icons look the same, and theoretically should have the same function, after spending a few minutes with the Illustrator version you realize that they are nothing alike. However, after understanding how Illustrator's peculiar version of slicing works, you'll be able to judge its strengths and weaknesses, and determine how to use Illustrator in your Web site creation workflow.

How Illustrator Slices

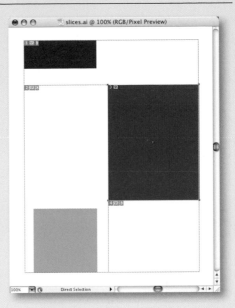

Illustrator slices are based on the dimensions of the artwork in your document. This includes objects on hidden layers, paths hidden by a clipping mask, or even objects with a no fill/stroke attribute. If you are used to the way slices are generated by Photoshop or ImageReady, it can be very disconcerting the first time you create a slice in Illustrator.

In this grouping of three rectangles, we selected the red rectangle and created an object slice from it. But instead of a single slice, Illustrator seemingly generated multiple unintended slices, which resulted in something resembling a bad Mondrian painting.

Slices By the Numbers

Slice Positioning

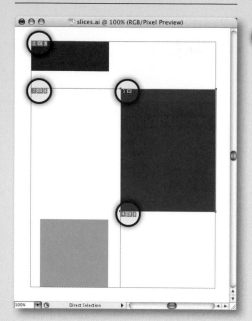

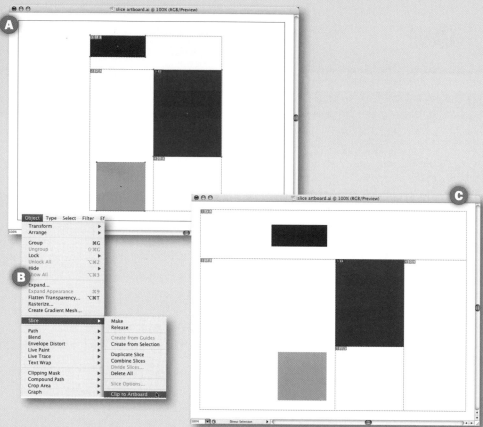

Slices 1, 2, and 4 are called auto slices and represent visual clues on how Illustrator has divided the objects on the artboard based on an HTML table. Slice 3 is the only selectable "user" slice in this file. Although very subtle, the active slice has a slightly darker outline than the inactive slices.

Slices are generated from the top-left corner (or *x, y* coordinate) of the topmost and leftmost object **A**. Any object or path on the artboard will be included in the coordinates of the slices. You can choose to crop the slices to the artboard by selecting Object > Slice > Clip to Artboard **B**. This will change the starting coordinate

to the top-left corner of the artboard and base the other slices on the artboard's width and height **C**. Any part of an object or path outside of the artboard will not be included in the slice(s).

For more on how to manage the positioning of your slices, see "Create a Web Layout" later in this chapter.

How to Slice

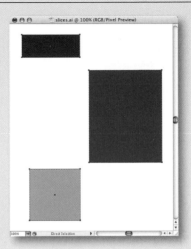

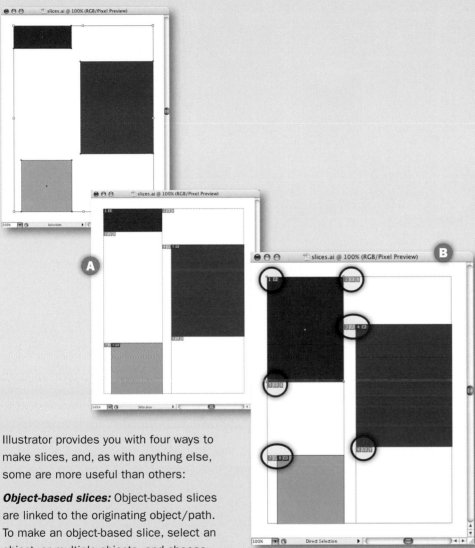

Illustrator provides you with four ways to make slices, and, as with anything else, some are more useful than others:

Object-based slices: Object-based slices are linked to the originating object/path. To make an object-based slice, select an object, or multiple objects, and choose Object > Slice > Make **A**. Using object-based slices comes in handy if you need precise width and height measurements for a slice or if you need to make multiple copies of the slice (see "Create Flexible Headlines" later in this chapter). Slices created using this method are dynamically resized, moved, and in some cases renumbered based on modifications to the original object **B**.

Slice from a selection: Creating a slice from a selection will generate a single slice from one or more selected objects. Unlike object-based slices, a slice made from a selection is not linked to the original object. To make this type of slice, select an object(s) and choose Object > Slice > Create from Selection.

How to Slice (continued)

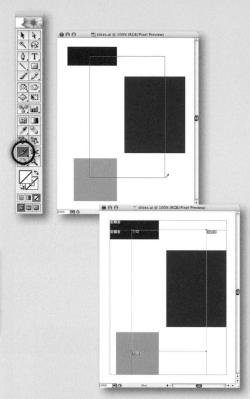

Slice from a guide: Creating a slice from a guide is similar to slice creation in Photoshop and ImageReady with one huge benefit. In Illustrator, guides aren't limited to vertical or horizontal lines pulled from the rulers (Cmd [Ctrl]-R). Since any object can be turned into a guide, you have many more options for how you create a slice.

Slice with the Slice tool: Using the Slice tool to create slices is crude and lacks any semblance of control, but it is a quick and dirty way to create multiple slices. You basically select the tool and start hacking away. In no time flat you'll have a series of slices that you'll probably need to go back and edit with the Slice Select tool. As you've probably guessed, with all the other options Illustrator provides to create clean, accurate slices, this method is not our favorite.

Moving and Deleting Slices

You can select any slice with the Slice Select tool and move it, but it's better to use the arrow keys. Make sure the Keyboard Increment in Preferences is set to 1 pt or 1 px to avoid any unintended half-unit measurements. Use the Slice Select tool to delete slices by selecting a slice with the tool and choosing Objects > Slice > Release or using the Delete (Backspace) key. For object-based slices you can simply delete the object, which will delete the slice too. ▨

Create Flexible Headlines

Create multiple headlines for a Web site with enough flexibility to change the colors or text without retargeting any of the image files.

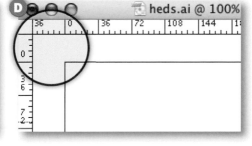

1. Set Up Your File for Slicing

When it comes to typographic handling, control, and speed, Illustrator leaves Photoshop and ImageReady in the dust. Consequently, creating headlines involving a lot of text using Illustrator is a smart choice. Create a new RGB document and set the artboard to 400 px wide x 1000 px high (this artboard size is arbitrary and is meant to give you a lot of breathing room if you decide to create several headlines) **A**. Remember to set the proper color settings for your file and enable Pixel Preview. For more on these steps, see "Set Up for the Web" earlier in this chapter.

Begin by setting the 0 point of your document. Either press Cmd (Ctrl)-R or choose View > Show Rulers **B**. When the rulers are visible, click the upper-left corner of the ruler **C** and drag the crosshair to the top-left corner of your artboard. This will ensure that the coordinates of your artboard's top-left corner are 0, 0. Any object or path created from now on will measure its coordinates from the top-left corner of the artboard, or 0 *x* and 0 *y* **D**.

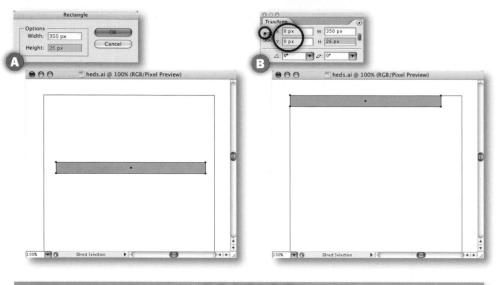

2. Create a Slice Rectangle

In this example, the available space for the image file (GIF or JPEG) is 350 px wide by 26 px high, so you need to create a rectangle with the same dimensions **A**. Keeping the width at 350 px wide enables you to create multiple headlines of varying text lengths.

Make sure that the rectangle has a fill but no stroke. See "Caution: Slices and Strokes" for more information.

With the rectangle selected go to the Transform or Control palette and click the top-left reference point. In the *x* field enter *0* and do the same for the *y* field **B**. This aligns the top-left corner of your rectangle to the top-left corner of the artboard.

CAUTION

Slices and Strokes. Using a rectangle with a stroke assigned to it can cause problems with the way Illustrator assigns a slice to that object (this "stroke" problem is also described in "Pixels, Points, and Strokes" earlier in this chapter). An object with a 1 pixel stroke actually falls a half pixel on either side of the path **C**. Illustrator then creates a slice adding a negative .5 to the *x* coordinate and a positive .5 to the *y* coordinate. Since slices are created based on a whole pixel (again, there is no such thing as a half pixel), the slice's *x, y* coordinates will be rounded up to −1 and 1, adding a full pixel to your object's dimensions **D**.

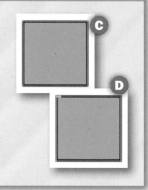

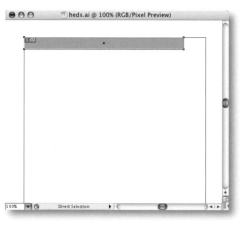

3. Create a Slice

Select the rectangle and choose Object > Slice > Make.

TIP

Hide the Artboard. For Web site design, many times it's best to hide the artboard to alleviate the visual clutter. Since there is no "edge" or trim to a Web site, and the 0, 0 point has already been set, there's no reason to view the boundary of the artboard at this point. To hide the artboard choose View > Hide Artboard.

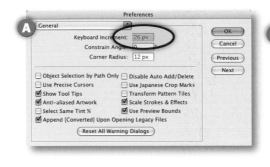
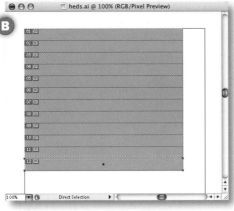

4. Duplicate the Slice

Open the Preferences dialog box (Cmd [Ctrl]-K) and in Keyboard Increment enter *26 px* **A**.

With the slice rectangle selected, hold down the Option (Alt) key while pressing the down arrow key. Since the rectangle is a 26 pixel-high object-based slice, the result will be the creation of slices stacked perfectly under each other in 26 pixel intervals. Repeat the last step 10 more times to create a total of twelve slices **B**.

5. Make a Slice Layer

Select all the rectangles, and in the Transparency palette type *30* for the Opacity setting. This gives the rectangles an opacity of 30% **A** and enables you to view how the slice rectangles relate to the headlines you will be creating. Lock the layer **B**.

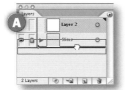

6. Set the Text

Create a new layer and drag it underneath the slice layer in the stacking order **A**. In the Character palette set the font to *20 pt* with a leading that is the same height as the slice/rectangle— *26 pt* **B**. On the new layer set the headline text so that it rests comfortably inside the top slice **C**.

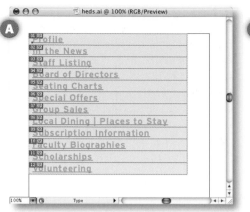

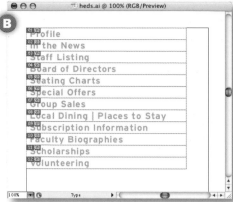

7. Create More Headers

On separate lines set more headline text **A**. At this point you can hide the "slice" layer in the Layers palette to get a better view of the headlines **B**. It's a good idea to name this layer so you can easily refer to it at a glance. If you need to modify the slices, the "slice" layer is only a click away.

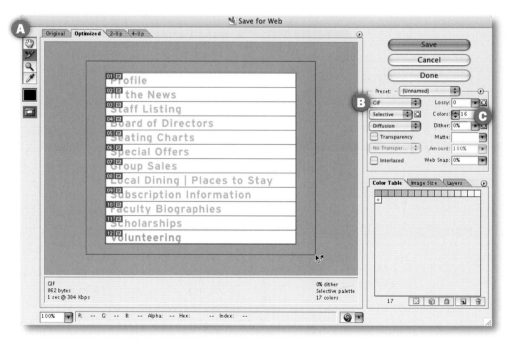

8. Export the files

Press Cmd-Option (Ctrl-Alt)-Shift-S (or choose File > Save for Web) to bring up the Save for Web dialog box **A**. Select all the slices by holding down the Shift key while selecting with the Slice Select tool, and specify the type of file (GIF, JPEG, or PNG) you want to save and at what quality. Since the image files will be based on text and not a photograph, the GIF file format is your best bet **B**. For the number of colors, choose 16 colors **C**. Click Save. For more on the Save for Web dialog box, see "Export with Save for Web" earlier in this chapter.

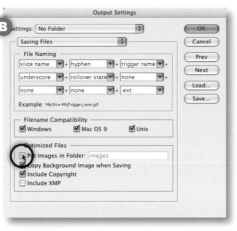

9. Save Optimized As

In the resulting Save Optimized As dialog box choose Images Only **A**. Under Settings choose Other, deselect the Put Images in Folder: Images check box in the Output Settings dialog box **B** (see "Tip: Dump the Images Folder"), and click OK. Back in the Save Optimized As dialog box, create a folder called "headlines" and save the files to that folder.

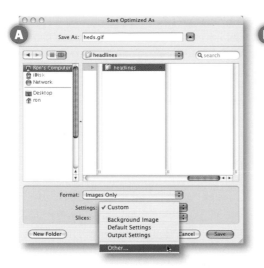

T I P

Dump the Images Folder. In the Save Optimized As dialog box (which appears after you click Save in the Save for Web dialog box), we make it habit to choose Other from the Settings menu, and then in the Output Settings dialog box go to Saving Files on the menu and deselect the Put Images in Folder: Images check box. We find this default setting very annoying because it always assumes that you want to dump all your images into a folder called "Images." If you are not careful, you can mistakenly create multiple "Images" folders and have a hard time locating your exported files. Instead, in the Save Optimized As dialog box choose or create the folder in which the files will be stored so there is no confusion.

10. Make Headlines Galore

Saving the files through the Save for Web dialog box will result in a series of GIF images named hed_01.gif, hed_02.gif, and hed_03.gif (based on the slice numbers) in a folder called "headlines" **A**. Now place these images into the Web site creation application you are using. Here we're using Dreamweaver **B**.

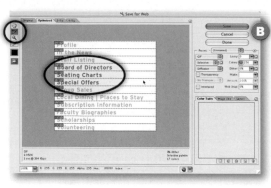

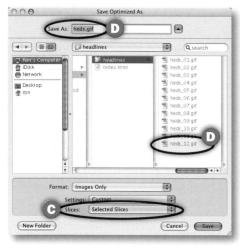

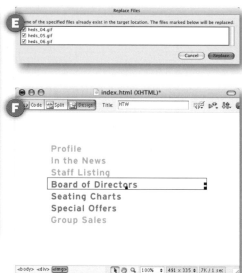

11. Change the Headline

Back in Illustrator, change the text color of three of the headlines and re-export them **A**. You can re-export all of them or just those selected **B** by choosing Selected Slices in the Slices option in the Save Optimized As dialog box **C**. Make sure you give the files the same names. However, be sure to exclude the number designation ("_01") since Illustrator will automatically assign the number "_01" based on the slice number. If you were to leave the number designation in the filename when you save the file, the resulting filename would be "heds_01_01.gif" **D**.

A Replace Files dialog box appears asking if you are sure you want to replace the files **E**. This is a good thing because it confirms that you are correctly replacing the same file(s) in the correct location. Click Replace.

Now when you return to your Dreamweaver site, all instances of these headlines will be updated automatically **F**.

Create a Web Layout

Use the precise tools in Illustrator to create a good foundation for a CSS Web site.

1. Set Up Your File

In this project, we'll create a Web site for Metrovation, a real estate developer. Prepare a document as described in "Set Up for the Web" earlier in this chapter and create a new RGB document with an artboard size of 800 px wide by 600 px high (the size of the Web site layout) **A**. Remember to enable Pixel Preview.

Next, set the 0 point of your document. Press Cmd (Ctrl)-R or choose View > Show Rulers. When the rulers are visible, click the upper-left corner of the ruler bar and drag the crosshair to the top-left corner of your artboard **B**. This ensures that the coordinates of your artboard's top-left corner are 0, 0 **C**. Any object or path created from now on will measure its coordinates from the top-left corner of the artboard, or 0 *x* and 0 *y*.

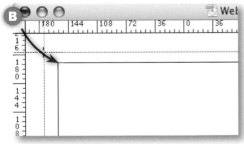

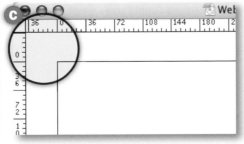

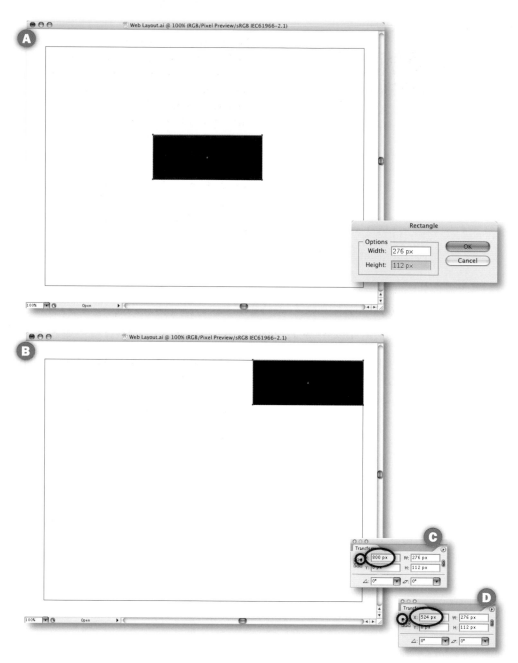

2. Lay Out the Page

One of the keys for successfully design-ing with CSS is planning your layout with numbers in mind. Creating div containers, floating columns, and all the elements that will fit into them requires precise measurements in pixels. This type of exactness makes Illustrator a great tool for CSS Web design.

With the Rectangle tool, click the art-board, and in the Rectangle dialog box create a rectangle 276 px wide by 112 px high **A**. The layout actually starts in the top-right corner. Using the Selection tool, choose the rectangle, and then go to the Transform palette (you can also use the Control palette) and select the top-right reference point **B**. In order to align the top-right edge of the rectangle with the top-right edge of the Web site layout, enter *800 px* for the *x*-coordinate and *0 px* for the *y*-coordinate **C**. Since the Web site dimensions are 800 px wide by 600 px high (as measured from the top-left corner of the artboard or 0, 0 point), the rectangle is now positioned properly. If you change the reference point of the rectangle to the top-*left* corner, you'll see that the *y*-coordinate is the same, but the *x*-coordinate is now 524 px **D** or 800 pixels (width of the Web site/artboard) minus 276 pixels of the object itself.

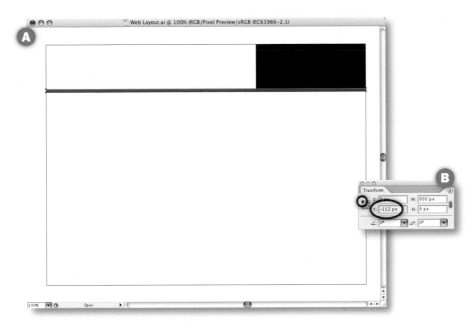

3. Add Other Objects

While creating your layout, make sure that no objects overlap, so you can click any object to get its exact measurements and coordinates. Using the Rectangle tool again, create the bar that goes under the top-right rectangle by clicking the artboard and making a bar 800 px wide by 8 px high **A**. Since the bar goes across the entire width of the Web site, its x-coordinate will be 0. The top-right rectangle is 112 px high, which makes the y-coordinate, as measured down from the top-left reference point of the bar, −112 px **B**.

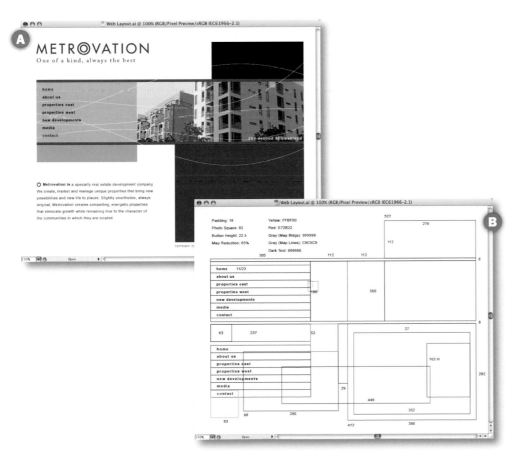

4. Complete the Layout and Make a Cheat Sheet

By using the same technique of measuring from different reference points in the Transform or Control palette, you can finish the basic structure of the Web site **A**. Create a new layer, and for your own reference, start to enter all measurements that you think you will need when you start to program the CSS code **B**. Also, enter any other specs such as main hexadecimal (Web) colors, stroke weights, fonts, and perhaps even phone numbers and e-mail addresses! Print this to use as a hard copy cheat sheet and then hide the layer.

5. Choose the Slices

At this point you need to make a few decisions about what you need in the way of image files and what sections you will re-create with CSS divs using the background color attribute. Once you identify that information you can create a new layer for your slices and place it on top of the other layers in the stacking order **A**. Select objects that need to be exported as a GIF or JPEG, and then copy (Cmd [Ctrl]-C) and use Paste in Front (Cmd [Ctrl]-F) to place the duplicated objects onto the new slice layer **B**. With the objects still selected, fill them with a common color and give them a 30% opacity so that you can visualize the relationship between the slices and the artwork **C**.

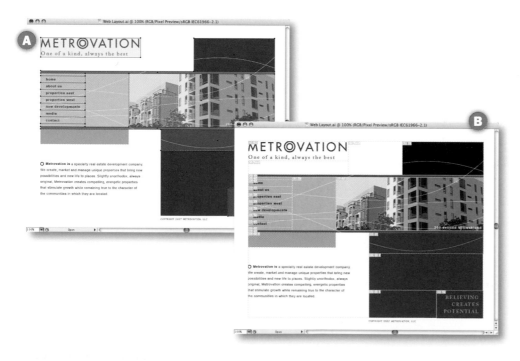

6. Make the Slices

From the base objects, you can modify and create other slice objects that you'll need for the page **A**. Once you are satisfied with the composition of the slices, select all the objects on the slice layer (Option [Alt]-click the layer in the Layers palette) and choose Object > Slice > Make **B**. After the slices are created, hide the layer unless you need to modify the slices later.

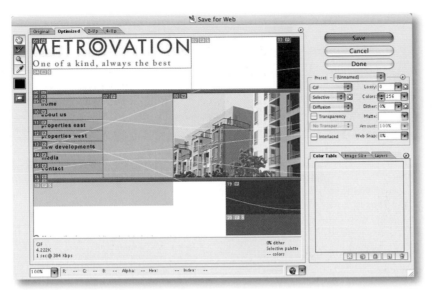

7. Export the Slices

Using the Save for Web dialog box (see "Export with Save for Web" earlier in this chapter), you can either export all the slices at one time or selectively choose sets of slices so that they can be saved to a particular folder or named in a certain way. For instance, you can save the menu buttons as a set. 🖐

T I P

Easy Rollovers. Creating different variations, or states, of menu images for creating rollover effects in applications such as Dreamweaver is easily done: Create a new layer, select the menu text, and Option (Alt)-drag the text in the Layers palette to the new layer **A**. Change the color of the text to the rollover color, and then hide the original text before exporting **B**.

Exporting to Flash

Successfully move your artwork from Illustrator to Flash by exporting a SWF file.

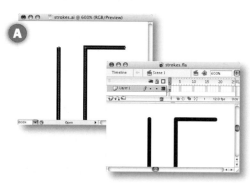

1. Outline Strokes

Cutting and pasting from Illustrator to Flash directly will give you wildly uneven results. Anything more than a single simple shape and your Illustrator artwork will look nothing like the original when pasted into Flash. One of the peculiarities of older versions of Flash is the program's inability to render strokes and corners without rounding them off **A**. Although this issue has been corrected in Flash 8 and the Flash 8 player through its Enhanced Stroke feature, until the Flash 8 player gains wider penetration in the market the problem still remains. The Flash 7 (and earlier) player doesn't support the Enhanced Stroke feature and will give you an error message if you try to export your file to older versions of the Flash plug-in (see "Caution: Enhanced Stroke Warning").

With this in mind, you first need to determine if your design or illustration has any stroke caps or corners, and then determine how detrimental the rounding of the stroke caps or corners are to your design. If you find the "rounding" unacceptable, it's best to outline those strokes (Object > Path > Outline Stroke), creating objects with clean, sharp edges **B**.

CAUTION

Enhanced Stroke Warning. When importing Illustrator files, Flash 8 automatically assumes that any strokes present in the imported Illustrator file have an Enhanced Stroke attribute. The Enhanced Stroke feature in Flash 8 gives you much more control over stroke caps and join types as well as numerous other improvements to how Flash renders strokes. However, if you try to create a Flash 7 (and earlier) SWF file, an error message appears in the Output panel since only Flash 8 (and later) players support the Enhanced Stroke feature **A**. To fix the Flash file so that this error message doesn't appear every time you preview or save a SWF file, save the Flash file (Save As) in the Flash MX 2004 file format **B**. When you return to the Flash file, the Enhanced Stroke attribute will have been removed from the Illustrator-imported strokes, and the error message won't appear again. The next time you save the Flash file it will automatically convert to the Flash 8 file format.

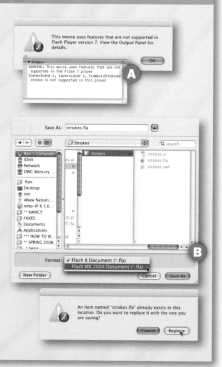

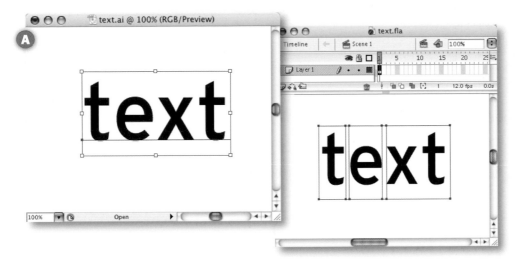

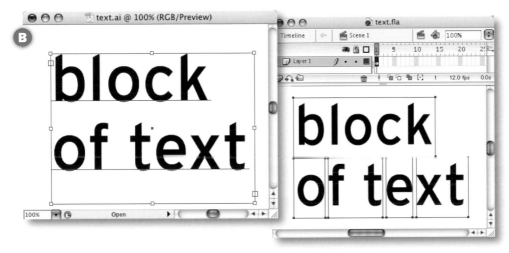

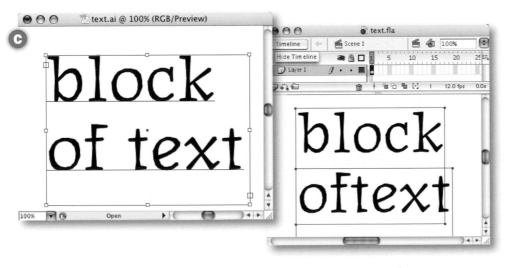

2. Outline Headline Text

Displaying Illustrator text in Flash is another instance where the two programs don't play well with each other. Exporting using the Export for Flash feature or copying and pasting a line or block of text directly from Illustrator to Flash will give you one of the following results. Note that each of these elements is fully editable:

A A line of text will be broken up into individual letterforms; at times two letterforms will be combined.

B A block of text will be broken up, but the first line of text isn't broken into individual letterforms and remains editable as a single block.

C A single block of text using the Journal font translates into two editable lines of text. The only problem is that for some reason Flash doesn't read the spacing character of this particular font!

To add to the confusion, there are times when exporting text (using File > Export > SWF) or copying and pasting from Illustrator works perfectly in Flash. As you can see, the results of importing text from Illustrator into Flash, whether through file export or the clipboard, is problematic to say the least. While not solving the problem, here are two workarounds to make moving the text in your artwork from Illustrator to Flash more manageable:

Outline heads: Outline the major headlines that depend on precise kerning and interaction with other elements of your design. This can also be done through the Macromedia Flash Format Options Export dialog box (explained later in the section "Flash Export Options") by either selecting Export Text as Outlines or Preserve Appearance (although the Preserve Appearance option might also

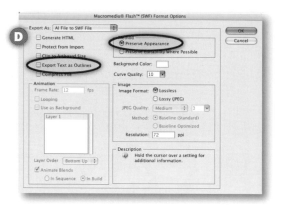

affect your other artwork). Using the Export dialog box keeps your original Illustrator artwork intact, but the downside is that you have no control over which text is outlined **D**.

Make a guide: Outline a sample text block in Illustrator and export it to Flash so that you can use it as a guide (font size, letterspacing, and leading), and then redo those text blocks in Flash for easy editing.

ILLUSTRATION BY CRAIG FRAZIER

3. Work with Masks

Although Flash supports masks, it doesn't translate Illustrator clipping masks very well. Illustrator artwork exported as a SWF file and imported into Flash will retain the hierarchy of the grouped mask object, but the clipping mask will be import as a nonfilled, nonstroked path **A**.

To fix this problem, select and then double-click the Flash group that contains the Illustrator imported artwork. Select the object that represents the imported clipping mask (it will be on its own layer) **B**. The mask on this layer will be grouped by default. *Do not* ungroup or break apart this object/mask! The mask has a fill and stroke of none, and if you break it apart, the path will disappear. Go into the grouped mask object. Select all (Cmd [Ctrl]-A) to find the path and use the Paint Bucket tool to fill the object with black (or any other color) **C**. When you exit the group, the mask will be working **D**.

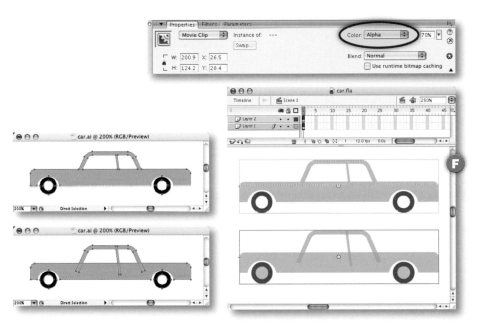

That's a lot of work! So you might be asking, isn't there an easier way? If preserving the clipping mask or the mask path isn't a priority for you, you can use Illustrator's Trim Pathfinder. This pathfinder eliminates the mask but preserves its appearance **E**. However, by using Trim Pathfinder you will also lose a lot of flexibility to modify your artwork. Also, remember that the Trim Pathfinder does not work on strokes (which will need to be outlined) or placed images. (For more about Pathfinders, see "Pathfinder Revealed" in Chapter 2, "Freeform Drawing and Geometric Shapes.")

Another advantage of using the Trim Pathfinder is when you want to apply an Alpha style to the symbol. In this example of two symbols with identical Alpha styles of 70%, you can see how a symbol created with overlapping layer objects displays differently than a symbol whose objects abut each other (via the Trim Pathfinder) **F**.

4. Hide or Delete Placed Images

Although Illustrator can easily handle placed RGB files, it's usually not a good idea to export them into Flash. You'll have much more control over size and quality by exporting RGB files through Photoshop or ImageReady, and then importing and composing them in Flash. That doesn't mean that all your hard work positioning your images with the text was in vain. Create a rectangle or holding area for your image, with the exact same dimensions and placement, and move this holding area to its own layer **A**. Now that you have an object that will act as a guide for placing your RGB artwork in Flash (you can also choose to use this object as a mask in Flash **B**), hide (or if you're really brave, delete) the placed RGB image.

5. Separate Your Work into Layers

At some point in the process of creating a Flash movie or site you will need to anticipate how to organize your work into layers. Illustrator is a much more friendly application for this purpose due to its superior selection tools (selecting multiple objects in Flash is not very intuitive to say the least) and the ability to move objects/paths between layers by dragging within the Layers palette. Moving all your elements to their own layers in Illustrator to create an overall template and then exporting the file to Flash is much easier than creating those layers in Flash.

For instance, you could move all your artwork (or holding areas for artwork) to a layer—separate from the text or headlines. Navigation buttons might be on their own layer as well as headlines, subheads, text, decoration, and so on. Interior pages could also be on their own layer.

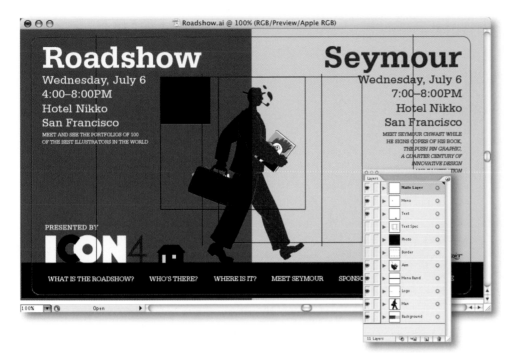

6. Show Pertinent Layers

After you have your design or artwork broken out into layers, all that's left is to export your artwork as a SWF file for importing into Flash.

Hide any layers of artwork not needed in Flash, including placed RGB images and redundant text. (For instance, if you have two inside pages with headlines that you re-create in Flash, you will only need one inside page to use as a guide for font size and positioning.)

Show any artwork that you will need for the Flash site. If an inside page layer overlaps a home page layer, that's okay. You'll end up separating them in Flash.

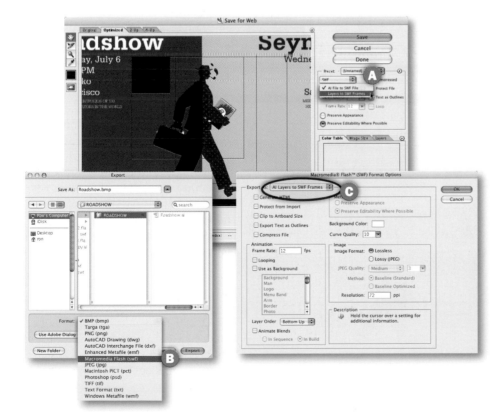

7. Export the SWF File

Export your Illustrator file to the SWF file format by pressing Cmd-Option (Ctrl-Alt)-Shift-S to display the Save for Web dialog box and choose SWF from the Preset menu **A** or choose File > Export > Macromedia Flash (swf) **B** which opens the Flash (SWF) Format Options dialog box.

We prefer the latter, because it gives you more options and isn't cluttered with choices that don't relate to SWF exportation. (For more information about the Flash Export dialog box, see "Flash Export Options" later in this chapter.)

For this example, you'll want to keep the layers intact, so choose Export As: AI Layers to SWF Frames **C**. Deselect Generate HTML since this is not the final destination of your artwork, and an HTML file wouldn't be of any use. Click Save, and then name and choose the location of your SWF file.

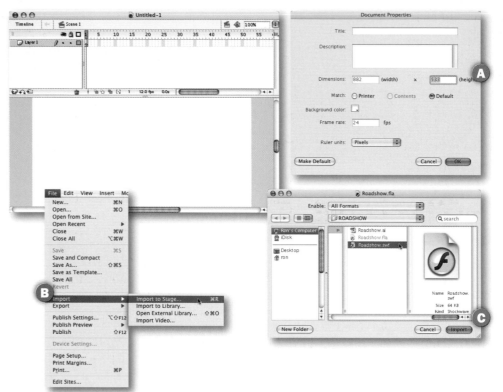

8. Import the SWF File into Flash

In Flash, create a new file with your final file dimensions—for this example, enter **882 px** as the width and **533 px** as the height (to change the file dimensions press Cmd [Ctrl]-J) **A**. Choose File > Import > Import to Stage **B**. Select the SWF file that was exported from Illustrator and click Import **C**.

9. Transition Files from Illustrator to Flash

When the imported artwork appears on the Stage, each imported Illustrator layer will occupy one frame in a single Flash layer on the Timeline **A**. If you scrub (drag the red square above the Timeline) through the Timeline, you will see all the artwork in each of the frames **B**. At this point you might be tempted to start selecting objects and move them into position on the Stage. *Don't!* One of the hardest things to do in Flash is to select multiple objects or symbols from different frames and move them at once. The following steps will help make the transition from Illustrator complete.

10. Convert Illustrator Layers to Flash

In Flash, create the same number of layers as there are frames (in this example, 10 layers total) **A**. In the Timeline, click and hold on the second frame (by clicking a frame in the Timeline all objects on that layer and frame are selected) and drag it to the layer you created above it **B**. Repeat until all the contents in the frames are repositioned onto different layers.

After all your exported Illustrator artwork is back into the proper layer order occupying a single frame, select all (Cmd [Ctrl]-A) and move your artwork to the correct position on the Stage **C**. With your layout from Illustrator transferred intact, you can start your work in Flash. ▥

Flash Export Options

The Flash Format Options dialog box, which appears when you choose File > Export > Macromedia Flash (swf), contains many more options than can be found in the Save for Web dialog box.

Anatomy of the Flash Format Options Dialog Box

A Export As: This menu gives you the option to save your Illustrator artwork in three ways: AI File to SWF File exports your artwork as a single SWF file; AI Layers to SWF Frames exports the layers in your Illustrator artwork to individual frames within a single SWF file; and AI Layers to SWF Files exports the layers in your Illustrator artwork to separate SWF files.

Remember, artwork that is hidden or is on hidden layers does not export.

B Generate HTML: This option creates a separate HTML file with code that references the exported SWF file, enabling you to preview the SWF file in a browser. The Generate HTML option comes in handy for quick previews of the SWF file or for generating the code for copying and pasting into hand-coding applications such as BBEdit. But if you are exporting the file for use in Flash or a Web creation program such as Dreamweaver, the HTML file is unnecessary and this option should be deselected.

C Protect from Import: This option prevents the resulting SWF file from being imported into the Flash application, thereby keeping others from tampering with it.

D Clip to Artboard Size: Normally, exporting an Illustrator file as a SWF file creates a document whose size is determined by the objects on the artboard. Using the Clip to Artboard Size option makes the exported document size the same as the dimensions of the artboard. Also, any objects completely outside the artboard will not be exported along with the other artwork. Objects partially outside the artboard will be exported in their entirety, although not visible if the exported SWF

file is viewed in the Flash player. However, if the SWF file is imported into the Flash application, the entire object will be visible and editable.

E Export Text as Outlines: This option outlines text for the exported file but leaves the original text in the Illustrator file unchanged.

F Compress File: This option makes the exported file size smaller but is irrelevant if the file is being imported into Flash.

G Frame Rate: At the top of the Animation panel (which is only active if AI Layers to SWF Frames is selected in the Export As option), the Frame Rate value controls the frames per second of the exported SWF file. If the file is being imported into Flash, the frame rate doesn't make any difference because the Flash application will set the frame rate.

H Looping: This option loops the animation but again is irrelevant if the file is being imported into Flash.

I Use as Background: By choosing this option and selecting one or more layers, the artwork on those layers will appear as a static background in *each* frame. If the exported file is not being imported into Flash, this option is useful for creating backgrounds for your animation. Otherwise, it's better to create a separate layer in Flash that contains the background and let it span multiple frames in the Timeline.

J Layer Order: By specifying either Bottom Up or Top Down, you can control the direction in which the animation plays.

K Animate Blends: Instead of animating via layers, this option animates blends in your artwork. The In Sequence option

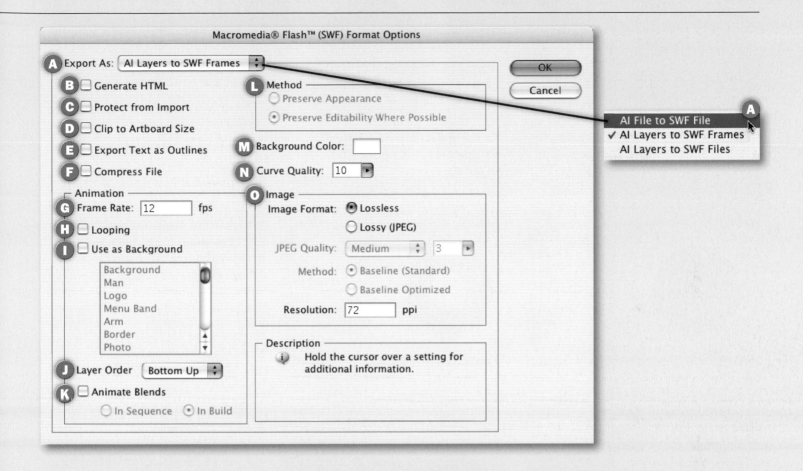

breaks up the blend (but leaves the original Illustrator artwork intact) and places each instance of the blend into individual frames. The In Build option adds the contents of a previous frame to the next frame. With the Build option a ten-step blend will produce a single object in the first frame and ten objects in the tenth frame, whereas the In Sequence option will produce ten frames with a single object in each.

Animate Blends is a handy option for simple objects, but more complex objects (such as art using the 3D filter) are best broken into layers first as outlined in "Create a Simple Flash Animation" later in this chapter.

L *Method:* Preserve Appearance flattens transparency or other special effects in Illustrator if necessary. Preserve Editability Where Possible is preferable if you plan on importing the SWF file into Flash. This option is only available when Export As: AI File to SWF File is chosen.

M *Background Color:* This option specifies the background color if the SWF file is the final destination. It is not applicable if the file is imported into Flash.

N *Curve Quality:* This option sets the smoothness of the curve in the SWF file. It is not applicable if the file is imported into Flash.

O *Image:* This panel determines how raster content in your file is handled during export. Using the Lossy (JPEG) option is obviously preferred if the SWF file is the final destination and you need to keep the file size as small as possible. Otherwise, if the file is being imported into Flash, Lossless is a good option since the raster optimization settings in Flash are superior to the options offered in this panel. ▥

Create a Simple Flash Animation

Produce a simple 3D animation in Illustrator that would be very difficult to execute in Flash.

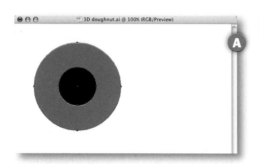

1. Create the Beginning and End Objects

Although animation through tweening or ActionScript in Flash is always preferable, there are instances where frame-by-frame animation can't be avoided. For this project we'll create a simple 3D doughnut that rotates on its axis. Create a filled circle with a smaller circle inside it **A**. Then select both objects and make a compound path by pressing Cmd (Ctrl)-8 **B**.

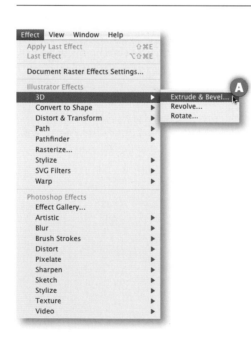

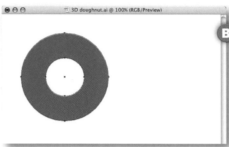

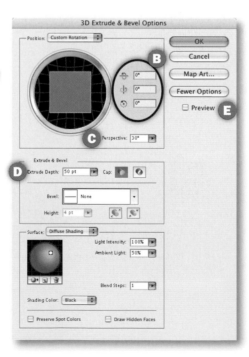

2. Add a 3D Effect

Select the "doughnut" compound path and choose Effect > 3D > Extrude & Bevel **A**. In the 3D Extrude & Bevel Options dialog box that appears, click the More Options button. Enter *0* for the *x*, *y*, and *z* axes **B**. This will give you a starting point of a flat doughnut. For Perspective, enter *30* **C** and for Extrude Depth enter *50 pt* **D**. Select the Preview check box **E** to see what you've done so far.

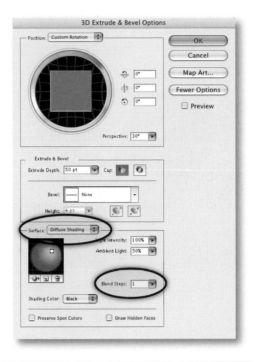

3. Illustrator's 3D Export Limitations

Although Diffuse and Plastic Shading might look pretty in Illustrator, due to the limitations of the export to Flash function, these shading options look downright awful in Flash. To lighten the processing load, choose Diffuse Shading from the Surface menu and enter **1** for the Blend Steps value. You can experiment by increasing the blending steps, but this one step is enough to convey a shadow for the 3D effect. Click OK.

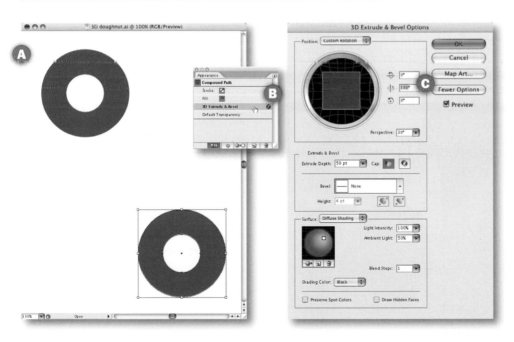

4. Duplicate the Doughnut and Change the Rotation

Select the 3D doughnut object and Option (Alt)-drag it to create a duplicate **A**. Change the rotation of the copied object by going to the Appearance palette and double-clicking 3D Extrude & Bevel **B**. The Options dialog box appears again. This time enter **180** for the *y* axis **C**. This will rotate the doughnut object to the other side of the flat doughnut. Click OK.

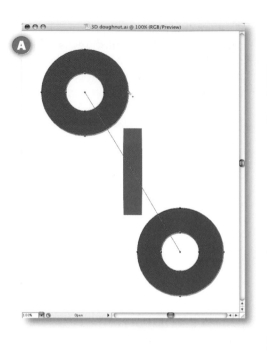

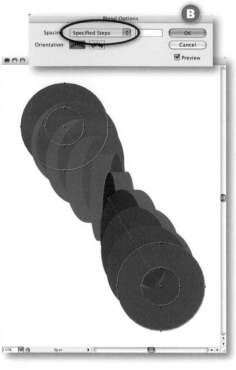

5. Blend the Shapes

Select both objects and press Cmd-Option (Ctrl-Alt)-B to blend the two doughnuts **A**. Select the Blend tool and Option (Alt)-click any of either the beginning or ending object's anchor points to bring up the Blend Options dialog box. For Spacing, choose Specified Steps and enter *8* **B**. Click OK.

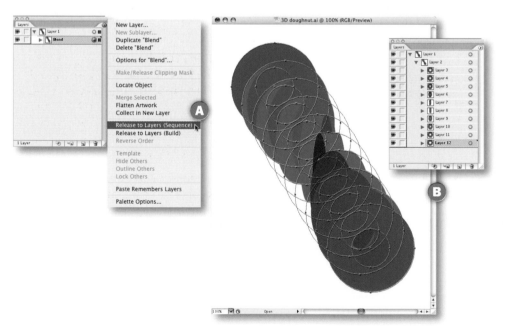

6. Release the Blend to Layers

In the Layers palette, click the disclosure triangle to view the contents of the layer. Click the Blend object in the Layers palette; it should be highlighted (you don't have to have anything selected on the artboard). From the Layers palette menu, choose Release to Layers (Sequence) **A**. Illustrator will automatically expand the blend and put the objects onto separate layers **B**.

7. Align the Objects

Align the objects into position by selecting all the objects, and then in the Align palette, click Horizontal and Vertical Align Center.

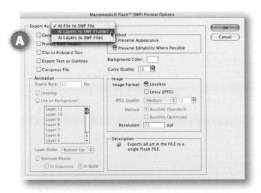

8. Export to Flash

Choose File > Export and select Macromedia Flash (SWF) as your file format. In the Flash (SWF) Format Options dialog box choose AI Layers to SWF Frames from the Export As menu **A**. If the resulting SWF file will be the final destination, choose a frame rate and select Looping in the Animation panel. If this file will be imported into Flash, you can disregard the Animation settings.

The result is a 3D shape rotated on its axis and a process that can be applied to other frame-by-frame Flash animations **B**. ⌘

7

INTEGRATING ILLUSTRATOR AND PHOTOSHOP

Combining Vector and Bitmap Images with Ease

GETTING ILLUSTRATOR ARTWORK INTO PHOTOSHOP *202*

GETTING PHOTOSHOP IMAGES INTO ILLUSTRATOR *206*

COLORIZING 1-BIT AND 8-BIT IMAGES *209*

CREATING A SMART OBJECT IN PHOTOSHOP *212*

USING ILLUSTRATOR WITH PHOTOGRAPHY *215*

WHEN IT COMES TO working together, Illustrator and Photoshop get along like two old friends. Besides the fact that these two programs share the same Adobe "look and feel," they also share many of the same tools and features such as the Pen and Type tools, paths, filters, layers, and so on. In fact, as time has passed, the two programs have become more and more alike. Photoshop now has vector-like drawing tools. Illustrator can create drop shadows, has true transparency, and includes Save for Web features. But as we know it's hard to do everything extremely well. And while these two programs have become the equivalent of a software Swiss army knife, Photoshop remains an image editor at heart, and Illustrator is still the program of choice for serious vector drawing.

Borrowing Benefits

Many projects tackled by illustrators, designers, and even the hobbyists involve a combination of illustrations, photographs, and type. Bringing images into Illustrator from Photoshop and integrating them with vector artwork can result in beautiful, multifaceted illustrations. In turn, many illustrators also turn to Photoshop to add elements such as textures, gradients, glows, and shadows to vector artwork. Another added benefit for importing Illustrator art into Photoshop is that many artists find it easier and less problematic to export from Photoshop for their final output. What's more, if you rasterize and flatten your Illustrator layers into a single layer, it prevents others from mucking with your artwork, ensuring it will appear as you want it.

Preserving Elements

Rest assured that moving artwork between the two programs is virtually problem free. Most elements, such as layers, layer comps, masks, paths, shapes, type, and transparency are preserved. But Illustrator can't support 16-bit images, so it converts them to 8-bit and flattens the file. For you videographers, it also cannot handle nonsquare pixels. Illustrator scales them to a 1:1 aspect ratio and again flattens the file. There are several ways to execute the transfer of artwork, depending on your particular needs. We'll show you all of the ways and let you take it from there.

> **TIP**
>
> **Photoshop File Formats.** Illustrator accepts the following file formats from Photoshop: TIFF, EPS, PSD, PDF, JPEG, GIF, PNG, BMP, FLM, PCX, and PICT.
>
> Photoshop accepts the following file formats from Illustrator: AI, PDF, EPS, PSD, TIFF, JPEG, GIF, BMP, PICT, PNG, and Targa.

Getting Illustrator Artwork into Photoshop

Depending on your needs, there are several ways to move Illustrator artwork into Photoshop. Do you need only part or all of the artwork? Do you want to retain the vector paths or rasterize them? We'll show you all the avenues to get there. You decide which road to take.

Exporting to Photoshop

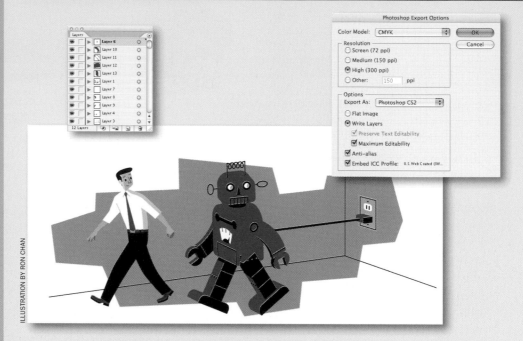

ILLUSTRATION BY RON CHAN

If you work with lots of layers in Illustrator and want to preserve them as much as possible when taking your artwork into Photoshop, Export is the command for you. In Illustrator, choose File > Export. From the Format pop-up menu choose Photoshop (psd). In the resulting Photoshop Export Options dialog box specify the following options:

Color Model: Specify a color mode of CMYK, RGB, or Grayscale for your exported art.

Resolution: Choose a resolution. Stick with 300 for printed output and 72 for Web images.

Export As: Stick with Photoshop CS2.

Flat Image: Merges all of your layers into one rasterized layer and does its best to preserve the appearance of the art.

Write Layers: Need layers? Then select this setting to export each top-level Illustrator layer as a Photoshop layer. Note, however, that Illustrator may flatten some layers to preserve appearance. Nested layers are flattened into the top-level layer unless you select the Maximum Editability option.

Preserve Text Editability: Exports point type to Photoshop type if artwork appearance allows for it.

Maximum Editability: Converts each top-level Illustrator sublayer to a Photoshop layer if appearance isn't compromised. The setting also goes beyond just layers

CAUTION

Preserve Maximum Editability. Always save your original illustration in the native AI file format to retain full editing capability later in Illustrator.

Set the Crop Area. Remember to set your crop area before exporting (see Chapter 1) to make it easier to go back and forth between Illustrator and Photoshop as explained later in this chapter in "Creating and Updating Artwork Based on Illustrator Files."

Exporting Layers. You don't have to export all your layers to Photoshop if you don't want to. Show only the layers you need in the Layers palette before exporting, and only those layers will show up in the resulting Photoshop file.

and tries to retain all of Illustrator's elements, such as Web slices, masks, and transparency. Note that Illustrator's compound shapes are converted into Photoshop shape layers, if at all possible.

Anti-alias: Slightly softens the edges of objects to eliminate jaggies.

Embed ICC Profile: Embeds a color profile. For more on color management, see Chapter 1, "Program Foundations."

Can't Convert Elements. If for whatever reason Illustrator can't convert certain elements of your artwork, it tries its best to preserve the appearance by merging the layers and/or rasterizing the vector art. This will obviously hinder full editing capabilities in Photoshop.

In Photoshop, choose File > Open. Select your Illustrator file and click Open. In the resulting Import PDF dialog box, specify your options such as how you want your image cropped, your desired resolution, color mode, and so forth. Resolution and color mode are critical, so be sure to choose the proper settings. As a rule, you should select CMYK color mode and a resolution of 2 x *your line screen* (line screen is usually between 133 and 188 lines per inch) for images to be printed. For images you intend to be viewed onscreen, use RGB color mode and 72 pixels per inch. Click OK. Your Illustrator artwork is rasterized and imported on a single layer. Because of this, be aware

that your editing capability is pretty limited. If you want the flexibility of being able to scale up your art later, you're better off dragging and dropping your artwork into Photoshop. Otherwise, you run the risk of serious image degradation as shown in the figures.

Two File Formats in One. You may wonder why in the heck you get an Import PDF dialog box when you're opening an Illustrator file. Native Illustrator (.ai) files have PDF files inside of them. It's like getting two file formats in one. It's a good idea to keep the Create PDF Compatible file option selected if you plan on opening your file in Photoshop.

Dragging and Dropping

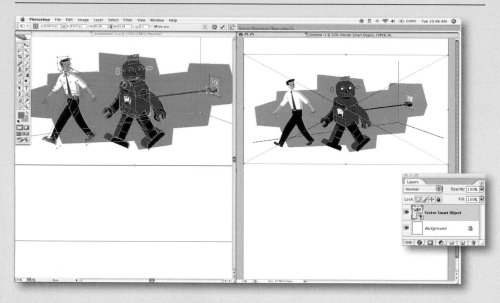

You also have the option of dragging and dropping your Illustrator artwork into Photoshop. Start by opening both your Illustrator file as well as your Photoshop image. Then select your Illustrator artwork. Drag and drop the art onto the Photoshop image window. When you see the black outline, release your mouse. The art appears inside a bounding box. Size and move your artwork as desired. When you're done, double-click inside the bounding box or click the Commit checkbox in the Options bar. In Photoshop CS2, your artwork will automatically be imported as a Vector Smart Object on its own layer. A Smart Object is basically a "container" that holds both raster and vector data. One of the great things about Smart Objects is, because the embedded data preserves its original properties, they allow for nondestructive transformations. In plain English, this means that

at any time you can scale, rotate, skew, and flip your art without any loss in quality. The other wonderful feature is that, like symbols in Illustrator, you can create multiple instances (copies) of the Smart Object. Edit one instance and all of the other instances are edited as well. This is extremely handy when creating repetitive artwork such as maps, guides, and tables. In addition, the Smart Object remains linked to the original Illustrator file so you can edit the vector data and it will dynamically update the raster data in the Smart Object. See the project "Creating a Smart Object in Photoshop" later in this chapter.

> **TIP**
>
> **Drag and Drop Paths.** To drag and drop your artwork into Photoshop as paths, hold down the Command (Mac) or Ctrl (Windows) key while dragging and dropping.

Copying and Pasting

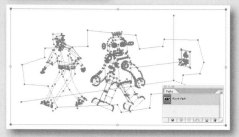

In Illustrator, select your artwork and choose Edit > Copy. In an open Photoshop file, choose Edit > Paste. In the Paste dialog box, choose whether you want to paste your artwork as a Smart Object, Pixels, Path, or Shape Layer. If you choose Smart Object, read the section "Dragging and Dropping" to learn how to finish the importing. If you choose Pixels, your artwork will import in a bounding box. Size and move your artwork as desired. Double-click inside the box when done. Your artwork is then rasterized at the resolution of the open Photoshop file and placed on a single layer. Remember, be careful when scaling up your art later or you will lose image quality. If you choose Path, as shown in the figure, Photoshop pastes the art as paths onto the selected layer or Background. You can then edit the paths with the Pen tools and Path and Direct Selection tools. If you choose Shape Layer, your artwork is pasted as a shape layer, which is a layer of color with an associated vector mask. Note that if your art consists of multiple paths, the resulting shape layer can be less than desirable. Vector masks allow for only a single color to be used per vector shape layer.

Setting Clipboard Preferences

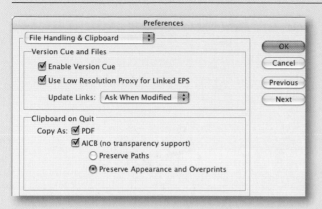

Placing a Native Illustrator File in Photoshop

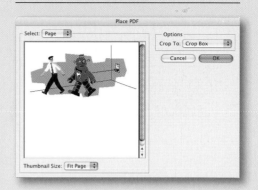

If you are using Mac OS X or Windows XP, running Illustrator and Photoshop simultaneously and copying and pasting between the two, you don't have to worry so much about your clipboard preferences. But you need to be aware of the preferences when you quit Illustrator with your data on the clipboard. Whenever you copy anything, Illustrator gets ready to store it on the clipboard. The program then copies the artwork in a particular way and gives you various pasting options (or not), depending on those preferences. Choose Illustrator > Preferences > File Handling & Clipboard (Edit > Preferences > File Handling & Clipboard). Here is a simple chart to guide your preference decisions:

Under the AICB option, if you select Preserve Paths, any transparency in your artwork will be ignored when copied. If you select Preserve Appearance and Overprints, your transparency will be retained, albeit flattened, and the overall appearance will be retained.

In Photoshop, choose File > Place and select your Illustrator file. Photoshop imports your artwork as a Smart Object. Refer to the section "Dragging and Dropping" to learn how to finish importing your image. Along with native AI files, you can also place Illustrator PDF and EPS files.

Illustrator and other Programs.
What about using Illustrator artwork in other programs besides Photoshop? Check out the section "Saving and Exporting from Illustrator" in Chapter 1 to find out the best file formats to use for some of the more popular applications.

PDF	AICB	Result
Unchecked	Unchecked	Pastes into Photoshop as a single rasterized layer
Checked	Unchecked	Pastes into Photoshop as a Smart Object
Unchecked	Checked	Paste dialog box enables you to choose from Smart Object, Pixels, Path, or Shape Layer
Checked	Checked	Paste dialog box enables you to choose from Smart Object, Pixels, Path, or Shape Layer

Getting Photoshop Images into Illustrator

Just as there are several ways to get Illustrator artwork into Photoshop, the opposite also holds true. You can open, place, copy and paste, or drag and drop. Depending on what you need, one method may be more advantageous than another. Regardless of your method, to ensure the best quality output, make sure your Photoshop image is at its final output resolution and dimension before importing it into Illustrator.

Placing a Photoshop Image in Illustrator

In Illustrator, choose File > Place to import the image. In the Place dialog box choose whether you want to link your image (see "Linking vs. Embedding" below). If you are embedding your file and that file contains layers, a Photoshop Import Options dialog box appears. You can choose Convert Photoshop layers to objects, which will retain the individual layers, masks, blend modes, and transparency. Adjustment layers or layer effects are rasterized. Or you can choose Flatten Photoshop layers to a single image, which will merge all of the layers, but will still retain any transparency. Type layers and layer effects are rasterized and are no longer editable. Layer masks are converted to Illustrator opacity masks. Other options include Import Hidden Layers, Import Image Maps, and Import Slices—all self-explanatory.

Linking vs. Embedding

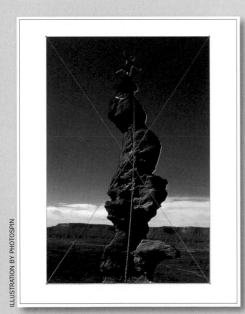

ILLUSTRATION BY PHOTOSPIN

When you import your Photoshop file into Illustrator as a link, the image remains independent from the Illustrator file. Illustrator imports a "proxy" or placeholder image and refers to the external Photoshop file where it resides on your hard drive or media. The advantage is that your Illustrator file remains small in size. The downside is that the Illustrator file will always need that link. If you move the original location of the link, you will have to "repair" or redirect Illustrator to the link's new location. If you accidentally delete the linked image, you will see nothing but the bounding box with an X through it. Another downside is that you are limited in your editing capability (can't edit the pixels) within

TIP

Using Low-Res FPOs. Placing high-resolution raster files into Illustrator comes at the price of lower performance and larger file sizes, which adds to the time the file needs to save—even if the raster file is linked and not embedded. Sometimes it's better to use a low-resolution (or FPO—For Position Only) version of the same file while you are working. Then when you are ready to output the final file, swap out the low-res file with a high-resolution version by selecting the low-res file, clicking the Relink button in the Links palette, and choosing the high-res version.

Illustrator. You can, however, edit the link in Photoshop by choosing Edit Original from the Links pop-up palette or by clicking the pencil icon in the lower-right corner of the Links palette. Note that you can link PSD, TIFF, PDF, EPS, JPEG, GIF, PNG, PICT, PCX, BMP, Pixar, and Targa file formats. If you embed the image, Illustrator copies the image data into the Illustrator file. The advantage is that you have more editing capability within Illustrator. The downside of course is that your Illustrator file will be much larger in size because of the inclusion of additional data. It also means that technically you will no longer need the actual Photoshop file. Don't trash the Photoshop file, however. If you ever want to edit the image, you'll need the actual file to do so.

ILLUSTRATION BY FHOTOSPIN

Opening a Photoshop Image in Illustrator

In Illustrator, choose File > Open and select your desired image. This command will create a new Illustrator file with the same name as the Photoshop file. It will also automatically embed the image into the Illustrator file. If your file contains layers, a Photoshop Import Options dialog box will appear. See "Placing a Photoshop Image in Illustrator" for details on options.

ILLUSTRATION BY PHOTOSPIN

Dragging and Dropping from Photoshop to Illustrator

You can also drag and drop a Photoshop image into Illustrator. Select your Background, layer, multiple layers, or selection in Photoshop. Choose the Move tool and drag the image from Photoshop onto your Illustrator artboard. Note that if you hold down the Shift key, your image will automatically be centered on the artboard.

Copying and Pasting a Photoshop Image into Illustrator

In Photoshop, choose Select > All on your desired layer (or Background if your image doesn't contain any layers). Then choose Edit > Copy. Note that you can also copy multiple layers. Display those you want to copy, hide those you don't, and choose Select > All and then Edit > Copy Merged. If you only want part of an image, make a selection and then choose Edit > Copy. Create a new Illustrator file using your desired dimensions. Choose Edit > Paste. Your Photoshop image will be embedded into the Illustrator file.

CAUTION	TIP
Getting Bogged Down with the Clipboard. When you copy an image, it takes up residence on your clipboard. Therefore, be careful when using this method with large, high-resolution images. Storing hefty files on your clipboard can bog down your system's performance. To rectify the problem, purge your clipboard by choosing Edit > Purge Clipboard in Photoshop.	**Copying Compound Shapes.** Note that you can copy and paste shape layers from Photoshop into Illustrator. After selecting your shape layer in the Layers palette, choose Select > All and then Edit > Copy. In your Illustrator document, select Edit > Paste. Choose between Shape Layer or Path in the Paste Options dialog box. Both options will preserve appearance and editability. Note that this works in reverse as well. See "Copying and Pasting" in the "Getting Illustrator Artwork into Photoshop" section.

Exporting Photoshop Paths to Illustrator

You can also export your Photoshop paths into an Illustrator file. For example, this can come in handy if you have created a path around an object within a photo and you want to use this path to combine it with your Illustrator artwork. Choose File > Export Paths to Illustrator. Choose a location, name the file, and click Save. In Illustrator, choose File > Open and select the path file. It then opens as a new Illustrator file.

You can also use the Path Selection tool or Direct Selection tool to select part or all of any paths in your Photoshop file. Either drag and drop or copy and paste the selected paths into your Illustrator file. If you copy and paste, choose whether to paste the path as a compound shape or compound path in the Paste Options dialog box. Pasting as a compound path is faster, but, occasionally, you may lose some editability. If you drag and drop, your path will be imported as a compound shape. ▥

ALL PHOTOS BY PHOTOSPIN

Colorizing 1-bit and 8-bit Images

Illustrator enables you to easily alter the color of your bitmap images.

1. Open Your Image

Open your desired photo in Photoshop. Crop and size your image to its final output dimension and resolution. If you want to colorize an 8-bit image, proceed to step 8.

2. Convert to Grayscale

If your image is in color, first choose Image > Mode > Grayscale.

3. Convert to Bitmap

Choose Image > Mode > Bitmap to convert your grayscale image to bitmap mode. Select your resolution and method of conversion. Each of the options will give you a different look. We recommend using 50% Threshold. Click OK.

4. Save the File

Choose File > Save, name the file, and choose TIFF from the Format pop-up menu. Click Save. In the TIFF Options dialog box, leave the defaults as is and click OK. Your image is now 1-bit TIFF, and all pixels are now either black or white.

5. Create a New Illustrator File

In Illustrator, create a new file with your desired color mode and dimensions.

6. Place the File

Choose File > Place and select your TIFF file. Decide whether you want to link or embed your TIFF (see "Linking vs. Embedding" earlier in the chapter). Either way, you'll be able to colorize it.

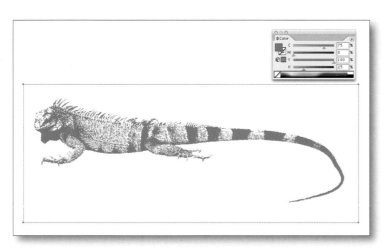

7. Choose Your Color

Select the image and choose your desired color from the Color or Swatches palette. Note that all white areas are transparent, enabling you to place your colorized TIFF over a background. Your 1-bit image is now colorized.

8. Colorize an 8-bit Image

If you want to colorize an 8-bit image, follow the preceding steps 1, 2, 4, 5, and 6. If you are working in Illustrator CS2, select the image and choose your desired color from the Color or Swatches palette. If you are working in earlier versions of Illustrator, you will have to create an opacity mask. See Chapter 3, "Masks and Blend Effects" for more on masks. ▥

ILLUSTRATION BY TIMOTHY COOK

Creating a Smart Object in Photoshop

A Smart Object is a container that embeds source raster and vector data.

1. Open or Create a File

In Photoshop, choose File > New and create a new blank canvas for your desired size, resolution, and color mode.

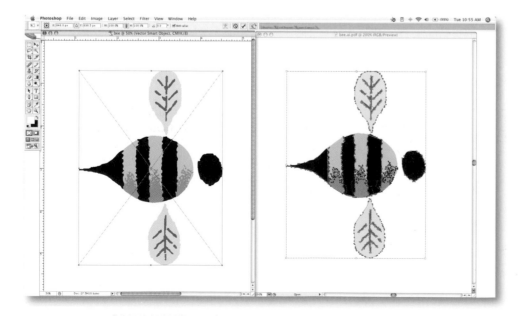

2. Import Your Artwork

In Illustrator, open your artwork. Drag and drop your artwork onto your Photoshop canvas. You can also import your artwork by choosing File > Place in Photoshop or copying and pasting from Illustrator to Photoshop. If you choose the latter, be sure to choose Smart Object in the Paste dialog box.

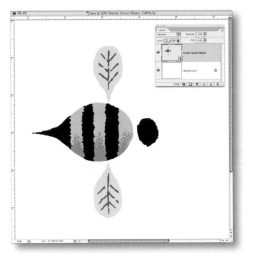

3. Size and Move Artwork

Size and move your artwork as desired. When you're done, double-click inside the bounding box or click the Commit checkbox in the Options bar. You'll notice a Smart Object icon on your layer thumbnail in the Layers palette.

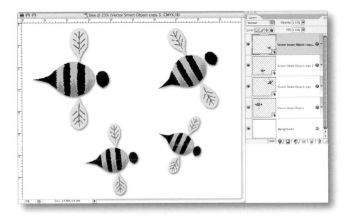

4. Duplicate Your Smart Object

Duplicate your Smart Object layer as many times as desired. Feel free to scale, rotate, skew, flip, or warp any of your Smart Object layers. You can also apply blend modes and layer effects.

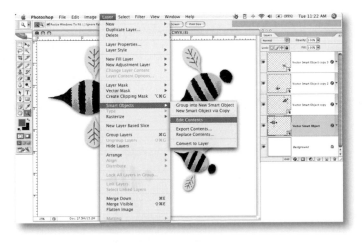

5. Choose Edit Content

To edit the vector data of your Smart Object, double-click any of the Smart Object thumbnails. You can also choose Layer > Smart Objects > Edit Contents. The Smart Object will then open in Illustrator. Photoshop uses Illustrator as the editing program.

6. Edit Your Smart Object, Save, and Then Close the File

Make all necessary edits to the Smart Object and choose File > Save. Also, be certain to keep the Photoshop file open while you edit the art in Illustrator. You don't want to break the link to the Photoshop Smart Object. If you do so, any changes will not be updated in the Photoshop file. Although it isn't mandatory, it's a good idea to close the Illustrator file.

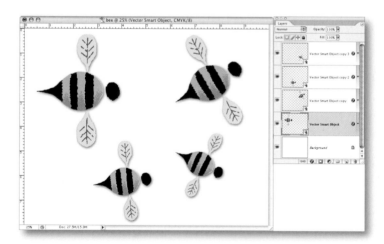

7. Return to Photoshop

Return to Photoshop. Give the program a couple of seconds to dynamically update all instances of the Smart Object in the Photoshop file. For more insight into Smart Objects, see "Dragging and Dropping" earlier in this chapter. ▥

Using Illustrator with Photography

Take flat vector Illustrator artwork into Photoshop to add texture and dimension.

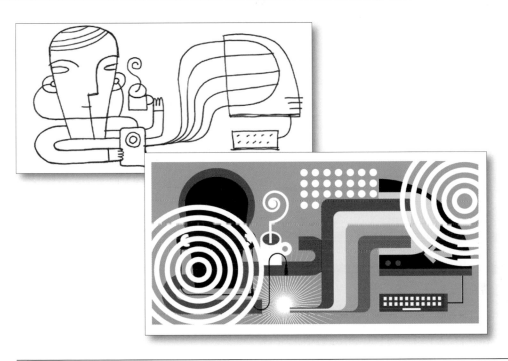

1. Create Your Illustration

In Illustrator, create your basic illustration, either as a composite or as individual components. Like many illustrators, Gordon Studer starts with a hand-drawn sketch, which he scans in and then uses as a guide for his Illustrator work.

2. Export Your Illustration to Photoshop

Choose File > Export. Select Photoshop (psd) from the Format pop-up menu. In the Photoshop Export Options dialog box, specify your desired color model, resolution, and additional options. For the greatest editing flexibility, be sure to select Write Layers and Maximum Editability.

3. Open Your Illustration in Photoshop

In Photoshop, choose File > Open and select your exported illustration. Note how the Illustrator layers are preserved to the best of Photoshop's ability.

4. Bring in Photos

Open your various photos, make your selections, and drag and drop them onto your illustration.

5. Add Photoshop Effects

Select your individual layers and add drop shadows, bevels, glows, and any other Photoshop effects. Effects can be applied by selecting Layer > Layer Style and then choosing your desired effect from the submenu. You can also create your effects from scratch as Gordon did with the shadows behind the hand on the iPod and the coffee steam.

6. Adjust Opacity

Select your individual layers and adjust the Opacity setting as desired. The Opacity setting is found in the Layers palette. Gordon uses a lot of varying opacities to create depth in his illustrations. For example, reduce the opacity on the concentric circles and dots to 26%.

7. Create Fades

You can have one layer fade or dissolve into another by creating a feathered selection or by adding a layer mask, such as the one Gordon used for the rainbow, shown in the finished illustration. ▦

Index

Watch over Jack's shoulder...

...as he leads you through over an hour of one-on-one Photoshop CS2 training—all from the comfort of your own desktop!

With the purchase of this book comes access to a sampling of the new high-quality streaming video instruction from Software Cinema and Peachpit Press with Jack Davis!

Learning Photoshop is now as easy as getting online. SOFTWARE CINEMA and PEACHPIT PRESS are pleased to introduce you to the newest and easiest way to master Photoshop CS2. Using new advances in streaming media, we are able to bring you Jack Davis' proven techniques in vivid, full-resolution detail. You will learn quickly and naturally as Jack walks you through each technique as if he were right there with you. As part of purchasing this *How to Wow* book, you can experience an hour-long sampling of these dynamic interactive Photoshop movies for yourself! Simply go to www.software-cinema.com/htw for log-in instructions.

Jack Davis has a knack for unlocking the hidden secrets of Photoshop—always with a practical emphasis on quality, flexibility and speed. In his *How to Wow* series for SOFTWARE CINEMA (with over 30 hours of instruction, organized into a set of four data DVDs), Jack holds nothing back. It's all here, every trick and technique (demonstrated in real time, in full resolution, with beautiful sound) that will get your images looking their creative best. From optimizing to combining to retouching, these are techniques you will use everyday! After learning Jack's mind-bogglingly easy and useful methods, you'll wonder how you ever handled Photoshop without them.

NOTE: Specific tutorial movies will differ from the examples shown here

Go to www.software-cinema.com/htw for more information on the *How to Wow: Photoshop for Photography* training DVDs, with over 30 hours of one-on-one instruction with **Jack Davis.** If you ever wished you could take a full semester class to learn Photoshop with Jack, here's your chance!

software **CINEMA**®
A Dean Collins Production